/1st (review copy) 6.50

JINGLE BELLS AND PASTRY SHELLS:

Holiday Baking Favorites for All Year Round

By Alma Smith Payne

PARTNERS IN SCIENCE

DISCOVERER OF THE UNSEEN WORLD:
A Biography of Antoni van Leeuwenhoek

with Robert Warner Chambers:

FROM CELL TO TEST TUBE

with Dorothy Callahan:

THE FAT AND SODIUM CONTROL COOKBOOK
(3rd edition of THE LOW SODIUM COOK BOOK)

THE GREAT NUTRITION PUZZLE

YOUNG AMERICA'S COOK BOOK

JINGLE BELLS AND PASTRY SHELLS:

Holiday Baking Favorites for All Year Round

ALMA SMITH PAYNE

Illustrated by Mae Gerhard

THE WORLD PUBLISHING COMPANY
CLEVELAND AND NEW YORK

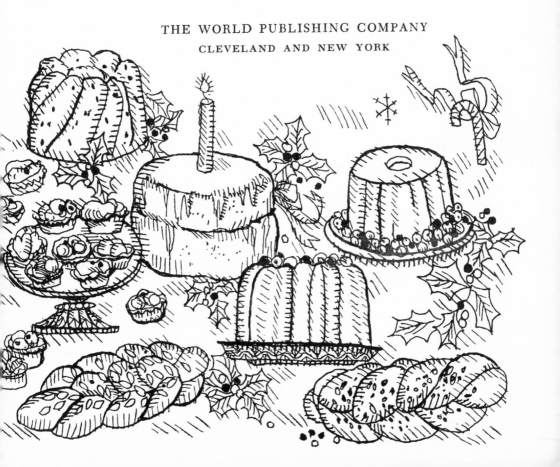

Published by The World Publishing Company
2231 West 110th Street, Cleveland, Ohio 44102
Published simultaneously in Canada by
Nelson, Foster & Scott Ltd.
Library of Congress catalog card number: 68-26982
Text copyright © 1968 by Alma Smith Payne
Illustrations copyright © 1968 by Mae Gerhard
WP
All rights reserved. No part of this book may be reproduced
in any form without written permission from the publisher, except for
brief passages included in a review appearing in a newspaper or magazine.
Printed in the United States of America.
Designed by Jack Jaget

FOR: *Dear friend Jane Zerga Voiles, essayist and former book reviewer of the* San Francisco Chronicle *and the* Saturday Review, *for her encouragement in this undertaking;*

My grandchildren, that they may appreciate and cherish the traditions and legends that enhance the enjoyment of "the glorious fumes of Christmas";

My husband, William R. Ralston, who by his patient test-tasting and critical evaluation of baked specialties and the written word helped me to complete this book.

Contents

CONTENTS

ACKNOWLEDGMENTS

I WISH TO THANK the following for permission to use recipes as indicated: Ray Farrow, Food Manager, and the Clift Hotel, San Francisco, for "Redwood Room Apple Pie," which appears on page 219; Mt. Vernon Ladies' Association of the Union for "Martha Washington's Great Cake," which appears on page 249; Saalfield Publishing Company for "Soft Ginger Cake," which appears on page 128, from *The White House Cook Book*, 1905 edition, by Hugo Ziemann and Mrs. F. L. Gillette.

Additionally I wish to thank the following for permission to use brief quotations: The Bethlehem, Pennsylvania, Chamber of Commerce for Moravian material on page 244; Charles Scribner's Sons for a verse from Eugene Field's "Apple Pie and Cheese"; David McKay, Inc., publishers of Harnett T. Kane's *The Southern Christmas Book*, 1958 (pages 238 and 239); Little, Brown & Company, publishers of *Herbs for the Kitchen* by Irma G. Mazza, 1947 (page 108); Atheneum, publishers of *The Margaret Rudkin Pepperidge Farm Cookbook* by Margaret Rudkin, 1963 (page 85); Charles Scribner's Sons, publishers of *Customs and Fashions of Old New England*, by Alice Morse Earle, 1893 (pages 226 and 244); The World Publishing Company for material on Dijon and the recipe for gingerbread as they appeared in *The Art of Eating* by M. F. K. Fisher, 1954.

I would like to acknowledge with gratitude the contributions of many other persons not otherwise acknowledged, and the typing of the manuscript by Edna Blackledge.

Last but not least, my special thanks to my editor Chaucy Bennetts for her enthusiasm and untiring work on the manuscript of *Jingle Bells and Pastry Shells: Holiday Baking Favorites for All Year Round*.

ALMA SMITH PAYNE

JINGLE BELLS AND PASTRY SHELLS:

Holiday Baking Favorites
for All Year Round

The Spirit of Christmas Past

MANY women go completely overboard about December entertaining and the preparation of their baked specialties, and I am one of them. The confusion this engenders acts as a tonic to my senses. I love to inhale the spicy fumes that permeate the house from the Monday after Thanksgiving until the very eve of Christmas as I make a variety of seasonal specialties. These include mincemeat; fruitcakes; tarts and pies, bulging with their fruited fillings; and an assortment of doughs and batters for Christmas breads, cookies, and cakes. Not all of these are for home use. Some are carefully packaged and sent to friends and family in faraway places.

A happy season anyway, Christmas is enhanced for me by the fond memories that crowd in at every step in the preparation of these festive baked treats—of my children helping me as soon as they were able, then learning to prepare these specialties themselves. They and their children after them—just as I did with my own mother and grandmother.

Like many other American and European women, I am a do-it-ahead and do-it-yourself person when it comes to the preparation of Christmas baked specialties. I like to be and I have to be, for I run a servantless house and have a penchant for December entertaining. Moreover, I know that many baked products are at their best only if made well ahead of use to allow them to "ripen."

Although I follow present customs and think I am quite modern, I cannot quite give up the weeks of Christmas baking in favor of today's excellent commercial offerings. In fact, I cherish with growing nostalgia the remembrances of such activities in my childhood, when Father, Mama, Grandma, my brother Buster, and various friends took part in the yearly mincing of fruits, stirring and beating of batters, and even in the baking of Mama's December specialties.

The passing years have made me realize my good fortune in growing up when the pace of living was slower. Then there was time for a little girl to be a part of all holiday food preparations and to learn, almost unknowingly, about the proud national traditions behind our seasonal breads, cakes and cookies, tarts and pies. And to begin the custom of collecting recipes.

My first recipes for Christmas baked specialties from various parts of the world came from the friends of those childhood days. Joe Bruno let me ride in his big Mack truck—and brought me a box of macaroons and delicious

Italian cookies from his wife's kitchen every December. The Herman Welcomes added German *Stollen, Springerle,* and *Mandeltorte* to my childhood vocabulary, after I sampled these and other fragrant German baked products in Mrs. Welcome's kitchen. Mrs. Finn Taaje told me of old Scandinavian Christmas customs as we made hundreds of Almond Balls, Swedish Spritsar, and Ginger Cakes. Later, my knowledge of holiday foods and customs was enriched by foreign students at the University of California.

Like Christmas dough expanding as the fermentation process does it chemical work, my file of foreign baked specialties expanded as my friendships widened. This book—a book both for those who like to read about food and for those who like to prepare it—is my treasury of Christmas recipes, customs, and legends, and I only wish I could have included them all.

While it could not be complete in its presentation of recipes or Christmas food beliefs and customs, it is representative of much that is fading from the contemporary celebration of Christmas, and I hope that it will encourage the continuation of these delightful traditions.

Many of the recipes come from my childhood—from my mother's and grandmother's kitchens. Others have been given to me by friends and family who have lived in various regions of our country or in faraway lands around the world, and who enjoy the rich scents of freshly baked Christmas foods. All of the recipes have been prepared in home kitchens. They do not represent *haute cuisine,* but they do have gourmet touches to distinguish them from the commonplace, and they are a planned blending of the old with the new. Some are very simple to prepare, and young people will find it rewarding to try them. Others require the skill of an experienced homemaker who cooks for "the love of cooking, and the joy of involving all of the family in the mincings and mixings."

Many of the old recipes have been updated to meet today's needs and to use new products. Where foreign recipes are used, necessary conversions to American products are used since our American products are sufficiently different from old-time European flours, baking powders, sugar, and butter as to necessitate certain changes in proportions of ingredients.

Some old recipes also have been reconstructed with substitute ingredients. The purists may shudder. I find the results satisfactory, I think my guests do, and I am sure the products are more healthful, particularly in a season when overeating is apt to be the rule rather than the exception.

The amount of saturated fat can be considerably controlled by the substitution of a highly unsaturated fat for a saturated one; in other words, margarine or vegetable oil for butter, nonfat milk for whole milk, and the increased use of egg whites instead of the whole egg in baked products.

When butter is the all-important ingredient of a particular recipe, use a little butter with the margarine, or simply use margarine or butter-flavored cooking oil to give the desired taste. Or use ½ teaspoon Ehler's imitation butter flavoring for each ½ cup margarine or oil, or "butter" baking pan with it and margarine.

My gauge is the finished product. Does it measure up to the original one? Is it pleasing to the palate in its new form? If it passes these tests, it stays in.

Of course in the reconstruction of recipes, specific arithmetical quantities are substituted for "a pinch" and "a teacupful," as careful measurements do pay good dividends.

Short cuts in preparation methods are also introduced. I am not one of those women who take two hours to beat and mix a poundcake when the modern mixer will accomplish it in thirty minutes. I believe in making my baking efforts count for family and guests and can see no reason for following the preparation steps of recipes invented before the introduction of the electric blender and mixer and other time-and-labor-saving equipment. My goal is flavor, not needless labor. I like to have enough energy left to have a good time at my own parties.

Trying to put all of this into a book has been an exciting adventure. Naturally I hope that each reader will be inspired to make these Christmas baked specialties in her [or his] own kitchen, and that the enjoyment of them will be enhanced by knowing something about the national origins, legends, and traditions of these very special dishes whether they are homemade or bought for happy December feasting.

OF FLOUR, MILK, AND LEAVENING

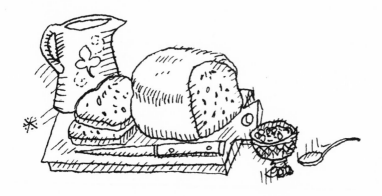

"The true housewife makes her bread the sovereign of her kitchen—its behests must be attended to in all critical points and moments, no matter what else is postponed."

—CATHARINE E. BEECHER AND
HARRIET BEECHER STOWE
in *The Housekeeper's Manual* (1878)

HOMEMADE bread went together with my childhood as naturally as thickly spread butter went with slices of Mama's freshly baked bread. Week after week Mama and I carefully measured and sifted various stone-ground flours taken from bins that hung like immense pendants below the marble-topped kitchen table which was the center of all baking activity. Week after week I helped Mama knead, pat, punch, and pull enormous mounds of dough, and waited for it to rise under the sprinkling of dry flour which topped it. Once the mixing had been completed and the sponge added, I kneaded and patted, punched and pulled those elastic mounds of dough until I thought I was the breadmaker, Mama, the helper.

December breadmaking followed the usual pattern, with one exception. We made many extra loaves of bread —little loaves and big loaves, long loaves and round ones, buns and rolls. The little round mounded loaves were my special delight for they were made of dough sweetened with sugar and honey, sometimes spiced with aromas as fragrant as Mama's rose garden in full bloom. They were decorated too—with frostings and candied fruits or nuts that dotted their tops like the multicolored pins that studded Mama's pincushion.

We gave these loaves of bread to neighbors and friends throughout the month of December, along with boxes of neatly packed cookies and little cakes, fragrant with spices, which in the making had converted our kitchen into a potpourri of scent.

As we baked in our ivory and green kitchen in Berkeley, Mama used her best kindergarten-teacher techniques to tell me stories about the foods and ingredients we were

using. She mixed customs and legends with history as artfully as she mixed her seasonings with basic ingredients. The expeditions of the Polo family, Vasco da Gama, Columbus, and Magellan came alive to me not at a schoolroom desk but in our California kitchen. Nor did Mama overlook the Bible and its many references to foods and their seasonings in the tales she told to spark my imagination and to increase my interest in foods—and perhaps to keep me a willing worker!

One of my favorite legends about bread has to do with the leavening of dough. It was said that Joseph and Mary, with the infant Jesus, took refuge in a farmhouse when they were fleeing from Herod's soldiers. They knew they must conceal the Child from their pursuers. They implored the farm woman to give them sanctuary. She looked up from her breadmaking and said, "I have no secret hiding place. We live in small quarters. Everything is in the open. I don't know how to help you." The parents looked at the huge mound of dough she was kneading and thrust the Child into the woman's doughy hands. Without a moment's hesitation the farm woman dropped the Babe into the dough and carefully covered Him with her mixture.

The soldiers arrived a moment later and demanded that she produce the Infant. They stomped through the house, ordering her to deliver the Child to them. The peasant woman did not look up from her kneading of the dough, nor did she speak as she gently pressed the dough this way and that. The parents blanched in fear that the Babe would cry out and reveal His hiding place. But He did not, and finally the soldiers went on their way.

When Mary lifted the Infant from the dough, a strange thing happened. The dough continued to rise, going higher and higher. It was as light as a feather. As the farm woman filled her baking dishes there was dough left over. Hearing of the miraculous quality of the dough, people came from near and far to get a piece of it to add to their flour-water mixes. And so it has continued from that day to this that some breadmakers save a small portion of their dough as a starter for the next rising.

In pre-Christian times one of the principal features of the winter solstice which took place in Julmond, the month of the yule, was the ritual that expressed reverence for the gift of bread and hope of the field gods' favor for a bountiful crop in the year to come. The sun gods were worshiped with elaborate ceremonies in southern Europe, Egypt, and Persia.

In Rome the festival known as the Saturnalia reigned for a week. In northern countries mid-December was a critical time for the crops as the days became shorter and the

sun weaker. As the days lengthened, there was great rejoicing among the people because of the promise of longer days and a stronger sun to follow. Thus the central idea of the winter solstice—the return of light—became the hope of the world in the birth of Christ, the Light of the World.

Invocations, display of wheat in homes, the baking of special kinds of breads and cakes, symbolic actions to ensure the fertility of the soil, honoring the spirits of ancestors, these and other customs were all part of early ritualistic observances which took place in the period that we now know as Christmas.

With the coming of Christianity many of these practices were discontinued. Gradually others were incorporated into the celebration of Christmas—the Mass of Christ— often taking on a Christian symbolism.

This secular and religious commingling has been preserved most clearly in the agricultural countries of Eastern Europe. For instance, in rural Poland sheaves of grain or wheat from the harvest decorate the four corners of the principal room in the house. Straw is scattered on the floor and table, and a cloth as white as December's snow is put over the table. Next the Christmas candle is put in place and foods made of traditional pastry are set upon the table as it is placed in front of the family shrine. All is in readiness for Christmas Eve.

The appearance of the first star in the sky signifies the end of the fast of Advent. The Christmas candle is lit, and all other lights are extinguished as the family kneels before the shrine to give thanks for its blessings. Then the father distributes the *Oplatki,* small white Christmas wafers which have been blessed by the village priest, to each member of the family. He kisses each person as he does this and wishes him a joyful feast. The dinner features special dishes and includes various kinds of fish, nuts, plums, and Christmas pastry known as *Strucle* and *Makowninki.* In the spirit of the season, a special place is set at the table for anyone who might knock at the door that night, an outgrowth of a still earlier belief that the Christ Child would be present in spirit to occupy it.

In old-time Ukraine wheat sheaves were stacked in the house as in Poland. Hay was strewn on the floor and was also scattered on the table. The table was decorated with two loaves of bread, one placed on top of the other, with a Christmas candle projecting from the top loaf.

The first and most important dish of the solemn Ukrainian Christmas Eve meal was *Kutya,* boiled wheat with honey and poppy seed. The father blessed it, then took a spoonful and threw it against the ceiling. This ancient rite, symbol of thanksgiving, has survived from the pre-Christian era.

Today much of our Christmas bread is made with cakes of yeast, instead of starter dough as in the dough and Christ Child legend. Nondescript in appearance, the little square of yeast is one of the wonders of the world. It moves mountains of dough, as Julian Street states in *Table Topics.* It is the leavener for Christmas breads throughout the civilized world, providing a base for a variety of seasonal specialties.

There is the German *Christstollen*—a large loaf of bread often shaped like a crescent or overgrown Parker House roll, bursting with raisins, candied fruits, citron, and almonds to give it special flavor and richness; the English fruit bread; the cakelike *Früchtenbrot* of Austria, which is served to bellringers on Christmas Eve as they go from house to house singing their carols, and is in fact served many times throughout the Christmas season in Austrian homes. The Netherlands, and Germany as well, give us *Kuchen*—coffeecake—like *Apfelkuchen,* old Dutch coffeecake; Sweden offers us its Lucia buns; Norway has its *Julekake,* a cardamom-flavored Christmas bread filled with candied fruits; while Hungary specializes in *Patko,* poppyseed crescents. Czechoslovakia is famous for its *Kolache,* delicious fruit-filled buns. Italy, particularly the region around Milan, is renowned for its *Panettone,* a raisin, citron, and nut-filled round loaf of bread. Among the nations of Central Europe *Kletzenbröt,* fruit bread, is a favorite Christmas specialty. Greece has its *Christopsomo,* or Christ bread, identified by a cross on the top of its round, anise-scented loaf, and often decorated with frosted symbols representing the family's occupations.

Denmark is known for its *Wienerbrød*, the pretzel-shaped, cardamom, raisin, almond-flavored holiday loaf.

The Christmas loaf, *Pain calendeau,* is still made in southern France. No one would think of eating a piece of this bread until the first quarter is given to a poor person. In France and French Canada homemakers usually make large batches of small round loaves, *Pain d'habitat,* in honor of the season, whether or not they make bread at any other time of the year. Every region has its special customs and folkways.

One unusual custom occurs in the little village of Solliesville, France, where the entire population gathers on Christmas Eve to partake of a special bread. Daniel J. Foley in *Christmas the World Over* recounts that twelve children are selected to represent the twelve apostles. Each one receives an *obol* (0.73 grams) of bread, meat, and candies as a symbol of the apostles. Then supper, known as *le réveillon* here as throughout all France, is offered to the important people of the community and to their guests. During the Mass, various villagers depict the characters of the manger scene.

In our own hemisphere Mexico gives us its crisp Christmas Eve fried cakes, *Buñuelos,* which are eaten plain or with a cinnamon and brown-sugar syrup. Chile has its *Pan de Pasqua,* a Christmas bread made in a round shape which is a favorite for Christmas morning breakfast. Ecuadorian housewives serve a brown-sugar bread at their festive meal, while in Colombia *Arepas* (flat corn cakes), with very slight flavor, are relished along with crisp *Buñuelos,* the Colombian version of the doughnut. Argentina has its *Pan Dulce,* sweet bread, similar to other national fruit-rich sweet breads.

Many of these special breads—rich in dried fruits, nuts, spices, and other seasonings, and topped with special glazes and decorations—can be found in bakeries in December. But there is a special satisfaction in having a few homemade specialties.

These breads as well as cookies and cakes often feature the almond. This favorite nut is used whole, chopped, or ground to a paste. History tells us that its use dates back to olden times when philologers affiliated "almond" with Ægmond, a proper name meaning "The Protecting Eye," or with *Al Monde,* meaning "Lord of the World," so that certain spiritual qualities have been attributed to it. The almond tree is mentioned in Genesis, and almonds figure among the fruits and nuts offered to Joseph.

People believed that by eating food that contained almonds they would fend off evil and have protection from unseen forces. With this in mind, homemakers added handfuls of almonds or worked almond paste into many of their breads, cookies, and cakes, or used them as a filling or topping for baked specialties. Such excellent flavor was produced from these additions that the almond was kept as a favorite seasoning in many Christmas doughs long after the symbolism was forgotten.

The specialties I have chosen for this section make excellent selections for December breakfasts, brunches, morning coffees, TV parties, and other gala occasions. (I use some of them almost every month of the year.) All of them feature yeast as the leavening agent—quick breads (those that do not require time for the dough to rise because they are not made with yeast) are listed separately. The breads featured first are a few excellent basic breads and some fancy ones redolent with spices, fruits, or other flavors, often topped with *Streusel*, a flour-sugar-cinnamon mix, or glazed and decorated to please the eye as well as the taste buds. Some are easy to make, others are more complicated.

Whether the loaf is plain or fancy, it is the result of these basic steps: the combination of ingredients in the right proportions; the proper fermentation of the dough; and the baking of it at the right temperature.

Most breads used to be made with whole-grain flours, honey, and sweet butter; now we are apt to use white flour, sugar, and margarine. As we have become accustomed to our bleached white flours and their superior keeping properties, white bread has outstripped all others in popularity in this country. Many homemakers feel that the most superior product, whether homemade or purchased, is made of enriched white flour. Actually when the outer coats and germ of the wheat grains are removed and flour is enriched, only a few of the nutrients which were removed in the refining process are replaced. So there is real reason to vary the choice of bread to include other kinds besides white whether you make or buy it for holiday use or for any other time of the year.

In general, 1 cupful of very finely milled whole-grain wheat flour may be substituted for 1 cupful of all-purpose white flour, or ¼ cupful wheat germ and ¾ cupful all-purpose flour for 1 cupful all-purpose flour.

For corn bread I use a water-ground corn meal, because the germ is retained. If you add oats to flour, use steel-cut rather than rolled oats as they have greater nutritional

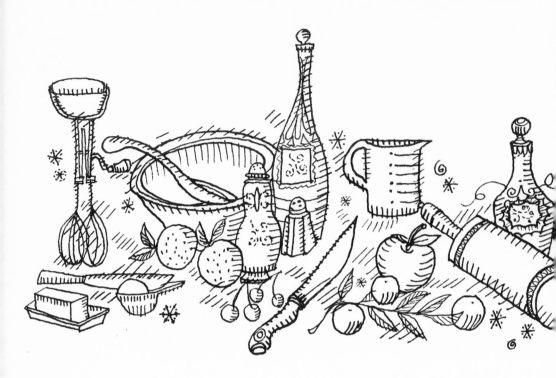

value. When you add any "improver" to your dough, such as wheat germ, dried fruits, or nuts, be sure not to use more than 25 per cent of the weight of the flour. Except for milk solids, such additions to the dough should be made last. Brewer's yeast, which has had a continuing vogue, may be added in the proportion of 1 teaspoonful to 1 cupful of all-purpose flour. Leftover cooked cereal may be added to bread doughs for added moistness.

ABOUT BASIC INGREDIENTS

It is important to choose the proper ingredients and to follow the recipe carefully to get the best results.

Before you begin your baking read the recipe carefully from beginning to end.

Check supplies to be sure you have all necessary in-

gredients and pans. Many recipes fail because they are baked in pans that are too small or too large for the mixture. A standard bread loaf pan is about 9 × 5 × 3 inches.

Use level measurements unless otherwise specified. In Christmas baking, with heavy demands upon spices, nuts, and other additives, graduated measuring cups and spoons are a great boon, and a strong, long-handled metal or wooden spoon is essential.

Unless otherwise stated, when eggs are an ingredient in the recipes in this book, large eggs are meant. Two egg whites may be substituted for one whole egg in most baked specialties, if desired.

Consider the leavening with special care. The leavening the recipe calls for is a very small part of the batter. Yet the right kind and amount of leavening used and the way it is blended with other ingredients can determine the grain, texture, shape, volume, and lightness of many a cake and other baked specialty.

For best results, follow directions exactly.

In recipes calling for margarine, do not use whipped types because most of them contain less fat per cup. But do use a polyunsaturated margarine. Do not substitute lard or vegetable shortening for margarine, since the fat content differs. One cup of lard is 220 grams; 1 cup margarine (or butter) 224 grams fat; 1 cup hydrogenated vegetable shortening is 188 grams; one cup vegetable oil is 210 grams. Use ⅞ cup oil for 1 cup butter or margarine in converting your own recipes to include vegetable oil shortening. Margarine does not have to be melted for ordinary use.

It is because the fat content of butter and margarine are the same and will produce the same texture, and because so many Christmas specialties are heavily flavored with spices anyway, that I think margarine can be used so successfully. See page 297 for additional reference to the substitution.

Shortening is added for flavor and tenderness, as well as an aid in browning, and to increase keeping quality. If the mixture is especially rich, as in many Christmas sweet breads which include eggs and more shortening than a standard loaf of bread contains, the action of the yeast will be slower. Sugar helps the dough to rise quickly, but too much slows the action of yeast. Of course the kind of flour influences rate of fermentation too.

Flour is the main ingredient in baked products. But there are many kinds of flour, and each has virtues worth considering. Unless otherwise specified, all-purpose wheat flour is used in these recipes. It is preferable to use unbleached flour for its rich nutritional value and excellent flavor.

If the recipe calls for sifted flour, sift before measuring. Instead of plain water, use milk or potato water (boiled, peeled potato mashed in water in which it has been boiled) for bread of better flavor. Fresh liquid milk, evaporated milk, and reconstituted milk (whole or nonfat) give satisfactory results. In recipes calling for yeast, milk should be warmed before using, to promote fermentation. Pasteurized milk need not be scalded and cooled before using, but raw milk must be scalded to destroy enzymes (which can affect yeast action).

Eggs are added to most Christmas breads for extra color, flavor, and to help make crusts fine and tender. Of course they add food value too.

If you are adapting your own recipes, use cake yeast and active dry yeast interchangeably. But active dry yeast can be added to the dry ingredients, whereas cake yeast must first be dissolved in water. The same amount of water is used with both types of yeast—only the water temperature and mixing methods are different.

All ingredients should be at room temperature, except soft margarine which may be taken from refrigerator and used immediately. Mixing bowls should be big enough to allow the dough to rise to twice its bulk. Rub bowl lightly with margarine or oil and let stand at room temperature while preparing dough.

After mixing and kneading, be sure to cover yeast dough with a slightly dampened cloth and let it rise in a warm place—80° to 85°—until double in bulk. (All temperatures in this book are Fahrenheit.) When dough is rising, keep it away from drafts, and be sure that bowl is well greased and the dough turned once so that greased side is on top to keep it soft and tender.

Whatever their national origins, festive coffeecakes and breads are made with a basic sweet dough plus special additions. Let us start with a labor-saving, quick-mix recipe for the basic dough. For best results, keep dough as soft as possible, almost sticky—just so you can handle it.

BASIC SWEET DOUGH
(New quick method)

4½ to 5 cups sifted flour
2 envelopes active dry yeast
½ cup sugar
2 teaspoons salt
¾ cup milk
½ cup water
½ cup margarine
2 eggs, or 1 egg and 2 egg whites

Thoroughly mix 1½ cups flour with undissolved yeast and other dry ingredients. Heat milk, water, and margarine over low heat until warm. (Margarine does not need to melt.) Gradually add liquids to dry ingredients. Beat two minutes at medium speed of electric mixer, scraping bowl as necessary. Add eggs and ½ cup flour. Beat for two minutes at high speed, scraping bowl occasionally. Stir in additional flour (2½ to 3 cups) until dough begins to leave the sides of mixing bowl. Then turn onto lightly floured board to knead. Knead dough about 10 minutes, until it becomes smooth and elastic. Place the dough in a lightly oiled large bowl, turning once to bring oiled side up. Cover with a dampened cloth and set aside in a warm place (80°–85°) until it has doubled in bulk (about 1 hour). Press two fingers into dough; they will leave an indentation when dough has doubled. Punch dough down by thrusting fist into center, pulling dough to center and turning over. Then return dough to bowl, cover, and let rise as before until it has almost doubled in bulk (30 to 45 minutes). After second rising, turn dough onto lightly floured board and divide it into portions for molding and shaping. Round up and let rest 10 minutes, so dough is easy to handle. Shape and let rise until light (15 to 30 minutes). Bake according to directions for desired type of bread, roll, or coffeecake as described in this section, or in a hot oven (400°) for 30 to 40 minutes.

Makes 1 coffeecake and 1 dozen rolls.

Sweet Breads From Far and Near

Austria THE MOST important family holiday in Austria is Christmas and it is celebrated from the time Saint Nicholas and his companion, Krampus, arrive early in December until Epiphany, January 6, when the Wise Men appear. Christmas Eve is heralded in many towns by the *Christkind Maerkte*, Christ Child markets, where *Krippen*, Nativity scenes, toys, Christmas tree decorations, and gingerbread are sold. The manger scene is the heart of Christmas decorations here as in Italy and many other European countries. Nearly every family owns hand-carved Nativity figures that are handed down from generation to generation.

The Christmas tree is very important in the celebration. Every town sets up a huge tree in an appropriate central place and sometimes there is an extra one decorated with breadcrumbs for the birds. For in Austria as in the northern countries in particular, birds and animals are thought to have the magical gift of speech on Christmas Eve and must be honored.

Many of the folkways date back to the Middle Ages
with certain adaptations to contemporary life. Austrian
Christmas folk music has rare charm and beauty. And it
was in the little Alpine village of Oberndorf in 1818 that
Franz Grüber, a schoolteacher, and Father Joseph Mohr,
the village priest, wrote the loved "Silent Night! Holy
Night!"

The singing of Christmas carols, attending midnight

Mass, and the enjoyment of good food are all part of the Austrian observance of Christmas.

Naturally in a country noted for its marvelous baked specialties there are many breads and rich coffeecakes that might be chosen as representative.

GUGELHUPF
Viennese Coffeecake

Rich and festive, this Viennese *Jause* (the equivalent of the English teacake) is suitable for your most gala occasion. Other popular Viennese coffee specialties include the Big Twist, Crumbcake, Poppy Seed Coffeecake, Walnut and Poppy Seed *Streusel* or Crescents, and Sugar Buns. Of them all, *Gugelhupf* seems to me to be the most unusual and delicious.

This recipe came to me from Shyrle Hacker, author of the delightful award-winning children's book *The Mystery of the Swan Ballet*, and was given to her by Frau Barbara Willman of Vienna. I am indebted to both of them for their permission to share it with you, and have adapted it for American usage and a quick way of mixing.

    3½ to 4 cups flour
    ½   cup sugar
    ⅓   cup powdered milk
    2   envelopes active dry yeast
    1   teaspoon salt
    ½   teaspoon nutmeg

1 teaspoon lemon peel, grated
½ cup (1 stick) softened margarine
1 cup very hot water
4 eggs, separated
½ cup seedless raisins, soaked and drained
⅓ cup blanched and halved almonds
  Confectioners' sugar

Be sure ingredients and equipment are at room temperature. Thoroughly mix 1 cup flour, sugar, powdered milk, yeast, salt, nutmeg, and lemon peel. Make a well in center and add margarine and *very hot* water. Beat 2 minutes at medium speed of electric mixer, scraping bowl occasionally. Add 4 egg yolks and ½ cup flour. Beat on high speed for 2 minutes. Stir in enough additional flour to make a soft dough. Fold in three egg whites beaten until stiff but not dry. Form batter into a ball and turn into a large oiled bowl. Turn batter over once so top is oiled. Cover with a damp cloth and let rise in a warm place (80°–85°) free from draft until double in size, about 1 hour. Thoroughly grease or oil and flour (or sprinkle with fine bread crumbs) the inside of a 2-quart *Gugelhupf* or Bundt pan or other fancy mold. Arrange the almonds to form stars or other pattern on bottom. Stir the batter down and beat vigorously. Add raisins and blend carefully. Pour into prepared pan. Batter should half-fill the baking mold. Let rise until doubled, about 1 hour. Brush top with remaining egg white. Bake in a moderate oven (350°) 50 to 60 minutes until it tests done. Invert at once, sprinkling lightly with sifted confectioners' sugar if desired.

Makes 1 large coffeecake (16 servings).

Czechoslovakia   The Christmas season in Czechoslovakia begins with Svaty Mikalas Day on December 6, and the holiday rituals associated with the feast of Saint Nicholas elsewhere in Europe are honored here. The religious observance is important. The Christmas tree is not. It is trimmed quite simply even now among the poorer families. Fruits such as pears, apples, and prunes; nuts; cookies cut in fancy shapes; gingerbread; paper and cloth cut-outs are typical decorations for it. However, with the development of the glass industry, glass ornaments of great beauty became popular, particularly in the cities, and were shipped in great numbers all over the world.

Since Christmas occurs so close to the winter solstice when night is longer than day, there is a popular saying in this country that "The day the Lord is born we are a flea's step ahead." Hence, here as in other countries where the old legends are kept in the remote and farming areas, there prevails a feeling that this is a time of promise for the days and year ahead. With the return of sunny days, a good time will be at hand for planting the crops to take the place of the disappearing winter food supply. Most of the old folk tales related to the success of the forthcoming harvest and the provision of an adequate food supply for the family.

Animals are not forgotten in the observance of Christmas in rural Czechoslovakia. A part of every dinner course on Christmas Day is taken out to them—to the hens so that they will lay all the eggs that will be needed; to the pigs so that they will grow fat; to the cows so that they will give sufficient milk for the family's needs. Nothing is wasted. In olden times even the bones from the meat course were taken out into the orchard and buried under the fruit trees to ensure a plentiful crop of fruit the following year.

Another old-time practice required the farmer's wife to

go out to the orchard and shake the trees, imploring them to bear a full yield in the year to come.

Incense was burned in the house and barn to keep evil spirits away. One old custom in Bohemia (as part of Czechoslovakia was formerly called) was a masquerade party; a similar custom is now observed at Shrovetide.

As in Poland and in parts of Germany, Czechoslovakians try to force cherry blossoms to bloom for Christmas. At the beginning of Advent, a cherry branch is cut and put into a jar of water in the kitchen where it is kept warm. This not only expresses the coming of spring and the promise of good things in the New Year, but if the branch blossoms on Christmas Eve it is said to bring special good fortune to the person who cut and cared for it; if unmarried, a woman will find a husband in the coming year.

Christmas foods are plentiful and varied in this little country. These include *Calta*, a plaited white bread which

is often called Bohemian Christmas Bread. Carp is an old-time favorite as well as *Cuba,* a pudding made of barley, milk, and mushrooms. A fruit stew called *Masica* is usually served with a slice of Christmas bread, and Kolache (*Koláče*), poppy seed or fruit-filled buns, are another specialty.

KOLACHE
Czechoslovakian Fruit Buns
Basic Sweet Dough (page 34)
1   egg
1   teaspoon grated lemon rind
½   teaspoon mace
    Marmalade, jam, fruit, Prune, or Poppy Seed Filling

To one-half recipe for Basic Sweet Dough add 1 egg, 1 teaspoon grated lemon rind, and ½ teaspoon mace. After second rising, make into assorted shapes (rectangles, balls, squares) by pinching off pieces of dough and shaping. Place on greased baking sheet 2 inches apart. Let rise again until light and almost doubled in size. Press thumb in center of each piece and fill cavity with marmalade, jam, Prune or Poppy Seed Filling. Bake in preheated hot oven (400°) 15 to 20 minutes. Remove from oven and cool on wire rack. Sprinkle top of Kolache with sieved confectioners' sugar.

Makes 30 buns.

POPPY SEED FILLING
½   cup poppy seeds
⅓   cup sour cream
1   tablespoon margarine
1   tablespoon honey
¼   cup almonds, chopped
½   teaspoon lemon rind, grated
1   tablespoon candied fruit

¼ cup seedless raisins
2 tablespoons sugar
1 tablespoon cornstarch
2 tablespoons currant jelly

Mix all ingredients in a large saucepan. Boil two minutes, stirring to avoid scorching. Cool, and fill dough cavities. Bake as described above.

For Prune Filling, coarsely chop 24 pitted, cooked prunes and add 1 tablespoon sugar, 1 tablespoon margarine, ½ teaspoon cinnamon, and ½ teaspoon vanilla.

GLAZE

Mix together 1 slightly beaten egg yolk and ½ cup water. Brush on sweet rolls before baking.

"Deck the halls with boughs of holly . . .
'Tis the season to be jolly"

England

The words of the beloved Christmas carol perfectly characterize old English Christmas traditions. Holly—thought to bring good luck to men—was considered a symbol of joy and merriment. Thus it was used to decorate old English homes to open the season of feasting, games, and good cheer.

Perhaps in your childhood, as in mine, reading aloud *A*

Christmas Carol by Dickens was as much a part of Christmas as the serving of traditional foods. In this and others of his writings Dickens became the English spokesman for the feast of Christmas in contrast to the religious fast that precedes it for the devout. Ivor Brown points out in *Dickens in His Time* that Dickens (like many Englishmen) enjoyed Christmas with all his heart and at the top of his voice.

I will have more to say about special feast dishes of the English home and other traditions in a later section. Now let me share with you one recipe for a fruit-rich English bread which I hope you will like. It was given to me by a superlative cook, Mrs. Marguerite Ingrim of Springfield, Illinois, and it is an interesting version of an old English Christmas bread because of its generous use of spices (not characteristic) and fruits.

ENGLISH CHRISTMAS BREAD

1   cup milk
1   cake yeast
½   cup butter or margarine
2   tablespoons sugar
3   cups flour
½   teaspoon salt
3   eggs or 1 egg and 4 egg whites
½   cup seeded raisins
½   cup chopped seedless raisins
½   cup washed and dried currants
1   tablespoon thinly shredded citron
1   teaspoon nutmeg
1   teaspoon cinnamon
½   teaspoon cloves
⅓   cup sugar

Heat milk to lukewarm, and crumble yeast into it. Add butter or margarine. Add sugar. Let stand until mixture is foamy (about 10 minutes). Sift and measure flour. Add salt, and sift into yeast mixture. Work into a rather soft dough. Add eggs one at a time, beating after each addition to blend. Cover with a damp cloth and set in a warm place (80°–85°). Let rise until double in bulk. Punch down; combine raisins, currants, citron, spices, and sugar and work into dough. Let rise again until light (about 20 minutes). Shape dough into a loaf, and put into a greased 9 × 5 × 3-inch pan. Let stand 15 minutes. Bake in preheated hot oven (400°) 30 to 40 minutes.

Makes 1 loaf.

For weeks before Christmas Day, German housewives busy themselves with the polishing of brass and silver and putting their homes in order for holiday festivities. They prepare a great variety of baked specialties for family and friends, for Christmas is celebrated with much gaiety and entertaining in the home, as well as with deep reverence in religious observances.   *Germany*

This accelerated activity actually commences with the beginning of Advent. This is the fourth Saturday, in Catholic homes, the fourth Sunday, in Protestant homes, before Christmas. On this day it is a widely observed custom to light the first of the four candles (three purple, one rose) on the Advent wreath, which is placed on a special table or hung from a ceiling beam in German homes. A second purple candle is lighted on the second Saturday or Sunday, and so on until the fourth Sunday, when the rose candle is lighted. Members of the family and friends sit about the wreath, singing Christmas carols or making gifts. On such occasions the homemakers proudly serve family and guests some of their rich fruited breads.

In towns and villages in northern Germany the Star of Seven—a seven-branched candelabra—is displayed in each home starting in early December. Lighted for the first time on Christmas Eve, the glowing "star" is carried across snow-covered fields or through forest lands to midnight service in the village church. Before the family goes to church, at five o'clock on Christmas Eve *Christstollen* is served, as it is from then on throughout the Christmas season.

Many of our finest traditional Christmas breads come from Germany, and *Christstollen* ranks high among them. There are regional differences in making this dough, and there are different ways of decorating it too. Some German *Hausfrauen* frost it with Confectioners' Sugar Icing (page 156).

Mother's old-time recipe called for brandy, cardamom, and mace as flavor additions, and I have always made it this way.

CHRISTSTOLLEN
German Christmas Bread

Basic Sweet Dough (page 34)
¼ teaspoon ground cardamom
¼ teaspoon mace
1 tablespoon brandy
½ cup cut-up blanched almonds and pecans
¼ cup cut-up candied cherries
¼ cup cut-up citron
¼ cup currants
2 teaspoons margarine
1 teaspoon butter

Add cardamom and mace to dry ingredients and brandy to liquids in making Basic Sweet Dough. After second rising, turn dough onto lightly floured board and flatten. Sprinkle nutmeats and fruit over dough and knead them into it. Pat out into an oval about 8 × 12 inches. Spread with soft margarine. Fold in two the long way and shape into a crescent or large Parker House roll. Press folded edge firmly in place so it can't spring open. Place on a lightly greased baking sheet. Brush top with a light coating of melted butter. Let rise in a warm place (80°–85°) until double in bulk (about 40 minutes). Bake in a preheated moderate oven (375°) 30 to 35 minutes.

Decorate with a sprinkling of sugar and fruits or frost with Confectioners' Sugar Icing (page 156) and decorate top with cherries and nuts.

Makes 1 large crescent or loaf.

December is the month of Saint Nicholas, patron of seamen. His *festa* is December 6 and is observed with great devotion in Greece. Because Saint Nicholas is master of the seas, no Greek ship travels without his icon on board. Seamen take to sea with them a dish of *kollyva*, boiled wheat grain. If the ship encounters bad weather and raging waters, they cast *kollyva* on the sea and say, "Dear Saint Nicholas, cease your rush."

Greece

Faith in the saint's miraculous powers has made his name popular throughout the country, and many churches are dedicated to him. Everywhere his icons are covered with silver tokens representing ships. Thus, in Greece, Saint Nicholas is much more important than a mere maker and distributor of gifts and goodies to children, as he is best known in the Western world.

The season is celebrated as a religious festival and many customs relate to the birth of Christ. At daybreak on Christmas morning, children in the villages go from house to house singing *kalanda* (carols), with the boys providing rhythmic accompaniment on their little metal triangles and tiny clay drums. The *kalanda* bring good wishes and praise for the master and mistress of the house, as well as announcing the birth of the Christ Child.

Christmas food in Greece is festive, with pork or chicken featured. Every housewife bakes a *Christopsomo* (Christ bread) which is decorated with elaborate frosted ornaments, usually representing some aspect of the family's occupation.

On Christmas Eve the Greek housewife places the Christmas loaf and a pot of honey on the dining table and arranges dried fruits, nuts, and sweets around it. The master of the house makes the sign of the cross over the loaf with his knife, wishes everyone joy and good health, and cuts the loaf, giving each member of the family a slice. After the ritual many other festive foods are served, varying according to the region.

In rural areas many practices center around the crops and are connected with the hearth. The plowshare and the Christmas table are placed near it. The table is set with the Christmas cake and surrounded with crop items and silver coins and a glass of wine in which the housewife dips the *Kallikantzaros* (goblin) buns. Everyone drinks wine, exchanges good wishes, and believes that this custom will protect the farm animals from evil, guarantee good crop yield, and bring good fortune to the family.

Dr. Kate Karakitsos of Athens took time from her busy medical practice to write me of some of the more important Greek observances I have noted and of special Christmas foods.

CHRISTOPSOMO
Greek Christmas Bread

Identified by a symbolic cross on the top, *Christopsomo* is a large, yeast-raised Christmas bread decorated with a cross outlined in walnut meats and elaborate frosted ornaments.

    Basic Sweet Dough (page 34)
2   teaspoons anise seed
9   candied cherries
1   egg white, lightly beaten
    Nutmeats, frosted ornaments, if desired

To Basic Sweet Dough add 2 teaspoons toasted anise seed. After the *first* rising, punch down dough and pinch off two pieces, each about 3 inches in diameter, and set aside. Knead remaining dough on unfloured board to make a smooth ball. Place on a greased baking sheet and flatten into an 8- to 9-inch round loaf.

Shape each of the 3-inch pieces of dough into a 14-inch-long rope by rolling out on board with the palm of hand. Cut a 5-inch slash into each end of the two ropes. Cross rope in their centers, but do not press down. Curl slashed sections away from center of each rope to form double circles at each ending of rope. Center each of these little cavities and center of rope crossing with a candied cherry, and brush the top of loaf lightly with a lightly beaten egg white. Cover loaf lightly, and let rise for about an hour until again almost doubled in size. Bake in a preheated moderate oven (350°) for 45 minutes. Test for doneness with a wooden pick in center of loaf. If it comes out clean, the bread is done. Decorate as desired. Serve hot, or cool on rack.

Makes 1 round loaf.

Hungary   Mrs. George Havas has shared with many of her San Francisco Bay Area friends tales of her childhood Christmases in Hungary. Christmas gifts did not come from Santa Claus on December twenty-fourth or twenty-fifth but between the late evening and early morning of December fifth and sixth, when children put their brightly polished shoes in the window before going to bed. On awakening they found them filled with simple sweets, dried fruits, nuts, perhaps a candy or two or a cooky.

Christmas giving was the privilege of the angels, according to Hungarian custom. Dressed in flowing white robes, and with mighty white wings and long flowing hair, angels supposedly flitted around in the mysterious twilight of pre-Christmas week, watching little children to see whether they were good or bad and marking their names in two books. One book was golden for good children's names, the other was black for the naughty ones. "Of course we never really saw the angels but every once in a while you were sure you had caught a glimpse of bright hair or white wings gliding past the windows," behind which the snow-covered trees made strange patterns as night descended.

Electricity was too expensive to be installed in Mrs. Havas' girlhood home, so the family gathered around the wood stove with its warm glow from the small iron side doors and told Christmas stories and guessed what the Christmas angel would bring. In livelier moments the children would take "trips" on coaches improvised out

of dining-room chairs. In the weeks before Christmas every free moment before twilight was spent on Christmas embroideries for the other members of the family. And the children learned Christmas poems and songs with which to serenade their parents on Christmas Eve. Poems, carols, and their embroideries were their channel of giving. "Money we seldom saw, but we could learn things to recite and we could make things . . . out of materials which somehow always appeared when we wanted to make some present."

A week before Christmas in this home as in others throughout Hungary, one door was locked and was heavily curtained—a sure sign that the angels were at work again! Excitement built up as the days passed until the solemnity of Christmas Eve afternoon finally came and the great bells of the church rang out into the crisp, cold winter air, calling all the townspeople to give first greeting to the Christ Child. At the conclusion of the five o'clock service, families rushed home to their snugly warm homes and to the mystery room. Its double doors were swung open to the tinkling of a tiny bell, a faint echo of the mighty church chimes.

There was "what we had waited for, the great, vigorous pine tree, tall and straight, from floor to ceiling, loaded with candy, cookies, red apples and gilded nuts, strands of golden garlands and fine angel hair; ablaze with the light of many small candles and sparklers. . . . I can still see the light of those candles reflected in the beloved faces as we stood around to sing 'Silent Night! Holy Night!' before finding little family gifts under the tree."

After every remembrance had been admired the "sweets of the Christmas tree were free prey for us."

Cookies and candies were by no means everyday fare in the lives of many Hungarian children, so it didn't take long for them to dispose of every edible ornament. Dinner followed, with roast goose, red cabbage, breads, and "the trimmings" featured. One wonders how they managed to eat so soon after the Christmas tree goodies.

When a child graduated from the mystery of the angels he joined the ranks of "the custodians of the great Secret." He shared in the baking and candymaking, the bustling preparations for December twenty-fourth. Sometimes he could stay up late and decorate the Christmas tree in secret with his parents behind the closed doors, "half elated, half sad at his privileged state."

Pusstabrot, the fennel-scented bread, *Mákos és Diós Kalács*, the Hungarian Christmas Bread, and *Keksz*, Christmas Tree Cookies, were all a part of Judith Havas' childhood, and she continues to serve them in her California home and to decorate her tree with *Keksz*, candies and nuts gaily wrapped for this special use.

MÁKOS ÉS DIÓS KALÁCS
Hungarian Christmas Bread

Like a jelly roll in appearance, this Hungarian Christmas Bread is particularly tasty because of the poppy seeds which flavor it.

½   cake yeast, or ½ envelope active dry yeast
⅔   cup lukewarm milk sweetened with 1 teaspoon sugar
1   cup margarine
¼   cup sugar
½   teaspoon salt
2½ cups sifted flour
1   cup poppy seeds
1   cup sugar
½   cup raisins
½   cup milk
    Grated rind of 1 lemon
1   egg, lightly beaten with 1 teaspoon water

Dissolve yeastcake for 10 minutes in lukewarm milk-sugar mixture. It will develop small bubbles when it is ready to be combined with other ingredients. Blend margarine, ¼ cup sugar, and salt in a large mixing bowl. Add flour alternately with yeast mixture or, if active dry yeast is used, combine with flour. Turn onto a floured board, correcting for flour to make a soft and manageable dough. Follow directions for Basic Sweet Dough (page 34) for kneading and first rising. Meanwhile combine poppy seeds and 1 cup of sugar with raisins, milk, and the grated lemon rind. Cook this mixture in the top of a double boiler over boiling water, stirring constantly, until it is of spreading consistency.

Divide the dough in half, punch it down, and roll each piece into a rectangle ¼ inch thick. Spread the rectangles with the poppy seed mixture and roll dough like a jelly roll. Place the rolls on a greased pan or baking sheet. Brush with egg and water mixture and let rise for 30 to 45 minutes, until almost doubled in bulk, then brush tops and sides of rolls again with beaten egg and water mixture. Bake in a preheated slow oven (325°) for about 40 minutes, or until rolls are golden brown. Slice as for jelly roll when ready to serve.

Makes 2 loaves 12 inches long.

The *presepio* or manger is the focal point of much of   ***Italy***
the Italian celebration of Christmas. You will find manger
scenes in homes and churches, from simplest presentation
of the Infant in his crib to elaborate and ornate displays
of village scenes around a manger.

This custom started on Christmas Eve in 1223 when
Francis of Assisi appeared before a great throng at the
hermitage at Greccio and celebrated the Mass on a manger
specially arranged by his friend Giovanni Vellita. It was
a moving experience for the friars and people of the Um-
brian hills as they gathered to pay homage to the living
spirit of the Infant born so many years before in the hay-
filled manger of Bethlehem.

Not only did Francis bring a new kind of glory to the
Christmas crib by his innovation, but he inspired crafts-
men to make miniature manger scenes for their own
homes. This interest spread over all Europe and before
long entire families were engaged in making figures from
wood or clay and arranging them to recreate the Bethlehem scene.

By the eighteenth century the creation of the *presepio*
had become a popular art. The Bourbon King Carlo III
took up the pastime with the enthusiastic cooperation of
the Queen and her ladies-in-waiting, who made costumes
for the various figures fashioned by the King himself. This
royal interest soon made the hobby a social custom, and
it became the talk of the kingdom. In Naples the *presepio*
was adorned with Neapolitan elegance.

Lesser folk also became interested in the crib through
the influence of the Dominican friar named Gregorio
Maria Rocco. He encouraged every family, no matter how
poor, to build a *presepio,* and he even helped some of his
parishioners to make them. And so over the years St.
Francis saw his wish fulfilled: that Christmas be a time of

devotion in every family in remembrance of Christ's birth.

But Christmas is by no means a somber time in Italy—quite the contrary. Bagpipe players march in the streets bringing their music to passers-by. Dressed in sheepskins they depict the shepherds who first came to see the Christ Child.

Christmas trees are not traditional in Italy, nor is the exchange of gifts on Christmas Day. This gift giving is reserved for Epiphany, when the Wise Men brought their gifts to the Child and when Befana makes her appearance in Italy.

Befana is the legendary old lady who supposedly refused to help the Wise Men find their way to Bethlehem at the time of Christ's birth. Later she repented and set out to overtake them, but she couldn't find them and is to be seen each year about Epiphany time wandering about the streets rewarding good children with little gifts and leaving switches for naughty ones. Unlike Saint Nicholas (Santa Claus), Befana is dressed simply and makes her visits quietly, filling stockings with candy or gifts for good children, with switches or pieces of coal for naughty ones.

Essentially Christmas is a religious and family observance, and there is an old saying in Italy that you may celebrate the New Year with whom you please, but Christmas only with the family.

No particular dish is common to all of Italy for Christmas. Special breads *Pan Dolce, Panettone,* and *Pan Forte,* however, are in great demand for this best loved of all holidays.

One of the best Christmas breads is *Panettone*—a golden, cakelike bread, rich and delicious. It is said that during December and until January sixth, when the yuletide season ends, Italians consume more than twenty-eight million pounds of their number one Christmas delicacy, first produced in Lombardy many centuries ago. There are

variations in the basic recipe for *Panettone,* but all resemble a kettle-shaped coffeecake, rich in citron, raisins,
and eggs. They come in every size from the tiny, *piccolis-
simo,* to the huge, *gigantesco,* for home use. Mounds of
Panettone are displayed in every pastry shop in Italy. And
they are popular host or hostess gifts. In Italy *Panettone*
is served at any hour of the day, before or after meals,
and with everything from coffee to Campari. I have seen
it served in our Italian restaurants as a high tubular cake,
a large wax candle burning in the center, no doubt to
honor a birthday. This cakelike *Panettone* is leavened with
baking powder and lacks the keeping quality of the recipe
I am giving you.

It is thought that *Panettone* dates back to fifteenth-
century Milan and the romance of the handsome noble-
man named Ughetto and the baker's blue-eyed daughter,
Adalgisa. When her father's business dwindled because
of competition, Ughetto took a job in his bakery to help
save the shop and to be nearer his sweetheart. He tried
to improve the baker's dough by experimenting with
various additives which he himself purchased out of his
own funds. No matter how he varied the ingredients—
butter, sugar, eggs, and candied citron, and basic sweet
dough—or how he shaped the dough, it lacked some
flavor he was seeking.

Finally on Christmas Eve he tossed in a couple of pounds of dried raisins, and at last produced the "perfect loaf." The pungent aroma from the Christmas Day baking of the new recipe for the festive bread brought success to the baker and a new delicacy to the people of Milan. Soon it became so famous that it was made throughout Lombardy.

After World War I, Angelo Motta, a daring maker of fine pastries, decided to make this old favorite in large quantities and to market it throughout Italy, according to Julia Cooley Altrocchi, who sent me this legend. Now it is available in the United States in all Italian delicatessens and in some supermarkets. It is increasing in popularity as more of us taste and know this famous round loaf.

PANETTONE
Italian Fruit Bread

2½ cups flour
¼ cup sugar
½ teaspoon salt
1 envelope active dry yeast
¾ cup milk
¼ cup water
¼ cup (½ stick) margarine
½ teaspoon anise extract, if desired
2 medium eggs or 1 egg and 2 egg whites
¼ cup seedless raisins
¼ cup seeded raisins
2 tablespoons chopped citron
2 tablespoons pine nuts
1 egg yolk
1 tablespoon water

In a large bowl mix together ⅔ cup of the flour, sugar, salt, and undissolved yeast. Combine milk, water, and margarine in a small pan and heat over low heat until liquids are warm. Then add anise extract. Gradually add warm liquids to dry ingredients and beat 2 minutes at medium speed of electric mixer, scraping sides of bowl as necessary. Add 2 eggs and ½ cup flour or more to make a soft batter. Beat this mixture at high speed 2 minutes, scraping sides of bowl as necessary. Stir in raisins, citron, and nuts. Add enough additional flour to make a soft dough. Turn out onto a lightly floured board, and knead until smooth and elastic (about 10 minutes). Place in greased bowl, turning dough once to grease top. Cover with a lightly dampened cloth, and let rise in warm place (80°–85°) until doubled in bulk (about 1 hour). Punch down dough. Cover and let rise again until almost double (about 30 minutes). Punch dough down again. Turn onto lightly floured board. Flatten with rolling pin, and shape as desired into the typical round loaf or Christmas tree. Put shaped loaf into a greased 3-quart earthenware casserole for the round loaf, onto a cooky sheet for the tree. Allow loaf to stand until doubled in size (about 40 minutes). Brush top of loaf with egg yolk diluted with water. Bake in a preheated moderate oven (350°) about 45 minutes, until golden brown. Remove from baking container and cool on rack.

Makes one 12-inch loaf.

Note: If you try a quick-bread *Panettone* made with baking powder, remember to bake it in a narrow or round deep metal mold; in a flat dish with a collar made of paper; or western fashion, in a small, buttered paper bag.

Kučia is the name the Lithuanians give their Christmas Eve supper. This features twelve traditional dishes or foods beginning with an appetizer of herrings, followed by beet soup with "little ears" floating on the top. Little ears are three-cornered pastries, filled with chopped mush- *Lithuania* rooms and onions, then boiled in hot bouillon. But before the homemaker drops the pastries into the soup, she expertly twists two points of the small triangles up and over to make saucy ears.

Pike is usually the main course. This may be followed by a salad, oatmeal pudding, and whole wheat bread lightly coated with honey and a sprinkling of poppy seeds. Fruit compotes and a fruited pudding come at the end, and of course there is some form of Christmas cheer.

The Lithuanians also honor the bounty of the crops in their home observances, and no Lithuanian Christmas Eve supper would be complete without *Preskučiai,* Christmas Eve biscuits, with a generous topping of *Aguonu pienas,* poppy-seed milk. *Preskučiai* are tiny biscuits which are put in a bowl. When they are served, a mixture of crushed poppy seeds, chopped almonds, and sweetened milk is poured over them.

You can serve these Christmas Eve biscuits as a novel dessert, or you may sprinkle unbaked dough with poppy seeds, bake and serve as an accompaniment to soups and salads.

PRESKUČIAI
Christmas Eve Biscuits

¾   cup nonfat milk
1   tablespoon honey
1   teaspoon salt
¼   cup warm water
1½ envelopes active dry yeast
2½ cups sifted whole wheat flour

Warm milk to 105°. In a large mixing bowl, combine warm milk, honey, salt, and water.

Mix yeast with flour and add to milk mixture in two additions, blending thoroughly after each addition until you have a firm dough. Form into a ball and place in an oiled bowl, turning once so that dough is oiled on top and bottom. Cover with a damp cloth and let rise in warm place (80°–85°) about 1 hour or until almost doubled in bulk. Turn out onto lightly floured board and roll into ½-inch-thick oblong. Cut into ½-inch strips and cut horizontally to make little squares, or shape into rounds. Bake in hot oven (400°) 8 to 10 minutes, until golden brown. Serve with Poppy Seed Milk.

Makes about 40 little biscuits.

POPPY SEED MILK

¼ cup poppy seeds
1 cup boiling water
½ cup almonds, blanched and finely chopped
½ cup sugar
½ cup milk
½ cup thin cream

If you cannot buy tiny poppy seeds, pulverize large ones in mortar. Cover with boiling water. Stir in chopped almonds. Add sugar. When cool, add milk and cream and stir. Pour over biscuits before serving.

Makes 6 servings.

Mexico The *Buñuelo* is the big fried cake that Mexicans traditionally serve at their Christmas Eve supper which follows the Mass of the Cock at the village church. In Mexican villages and in many parts of southwestern United States, where the Mexican influence is felt, other special baked treats are served during the festival of *Las Posadas*. This is held on nine successive evenings, beginning December 16, and commemorates the time it took Mary and Joseph to journey from Nazareth to Bethlehem. At nightfall a candle-lit procession is formed, composed primarily of women and headed by two children or by a man and a woman carrying a small platform adorned with figures of Mary and Joseph.

The celebrants go to a designated home each evening, where they beg admission. At first this is refused. Finally permission is granted and all join in the ritual of worship before an improvised altar on which the images have been placed. Suddenly the prayers cease and the gay *piñata* song is heard, whereupon the husbands and some of the worshiping women (who have been waiting outside) are invited into the house.

Refreshments are served. Finally a *piñata,* a crockery urn or jar, is broken by poles which are tapped against it by blindfolded children. This is the signal for the distribution of gifts to the assembled guests.

The last *posada* is held on Christmas Eve, *La Noche Buena.* Women prepare for the celebration of the birth of Christ by fashioning a shrine of December-blooming flowers, such as the native poinsettias, and cedar boughs. At midnight the image of the newborn Christ (in the form of a small doll) is placed in a manger.

Although the religious aspect of Christmas was and still is of great importance to Mexicans, they are such a gay and fun-loving people that many Christmas customs reveal their joy in color and pageantry. Fireworks, feasting, and frivolity, the display of the bright red, green, and white Mexican flag, candlelight and mellowed light from *luminarios,* or lanterns, mingle with the religious celebrations of Christmas to make it a time of unusual reverence and revelry.

At the stroke of midnight on Christmas Eve everyone rushes into the churches to celebrate the Mass of the Cock. The midnight Mass was so named hundreds of years ago because legend has it that it was the cock who crowed the announcement of the birth of the Babe in Bethlehem.

As the church service ends, families hurry out into the happy confusion of the streets to go home for a special late supper. Many specialties are served with pride. Whatever the choices, there are always *Buñuelos,* the festival fried cakes that are puffed, golden brown, and a great delicacy.

Instead of the traditional fried *Buñuelos,* listed below is an old recipe that my father brought from Mexico many years ago. It is a Mexican sweet bread that may be made into two delicacies for December entertaining. It is quite likely that it is still served at some of the *posada* gatherings.

BIZCOCHUELOS
Mexican Sweet Bread

- 2 envelopes active dry yeast, or 2 cakes yeast
- 2 tablespoons sugar
- 2 cups lukewarm water
- 6 cups flour
- ½ cup softened lard
- 1½ cups sugar
- 2 eggs, well beaten
- 1 teaspoon salt
- 1½ teaspoons anise seed
- 4 tablespoons brown sugar (reserve for *Ballos*)
  Melted butter

Dissolve yeast and 2 tablespoons sugar in lukewarm (warm for active dry yeast) water in a large mixing bowl. Stir in 3 cups flour to make a sponge. Beat until mixture is smooth. Cover with cloth and allow to rise in a warm place for about 1½ hours.

Cream lard and sugar, and add to dough with beaten eggs, salt, anise seed, and rest of flour, or enough to make a *firm* dough. Beat thoroughly, and turn onto a lightly floured board. Knead until smooth and elastic (about 10 minutes). Form into a slightly flattened ball, and place in greased bowl. Turn over once so greased side is on top. Cover with a damp cloth and set in warm place (80°–85°) until almost doubled in bulk (about 2 hours). Punch down and let rest (about 5 minutes). Divide in half, shaping one half in the usual way for a loaf of bread. Place in a greased 9 × 5 × 3 bread pan. Let rise until light and almost doubled in bulk. Bake in a preheated moderate (375°) oven for 10 minutes; lower temperature to 350° and bake for 30 to 40 minutes until bread springs back when tested. Remove from oven and brush top with melted butter or margarine. Let cool before slicing.

Makes 1 loaf.

BALLOS
Mexican Sweet Buns

In the Mexico of Papa's young adult years, *Ballos* were served with hot chocolate throughout the Christmas season. Sometimes they were sliced in two, brushed with butter, and sprinkled with sugar and cinnamon.

To make these sweet buns, shape remaining half of dough from *Bizcochuelos* into small balls, and place in well-greased muffin pans. Cover and let rise until light and a small indentation remains when pressed with finger (this will be in about 1 hour). Brush tops lightly with melted butter or margarine and press 1 teaspoon brown sugar into top of each bun. Bake in a preheated moderate (375°) oven 20 minutes or until golden brown.

Makes 12 sweet buns.

In Norway old beliefs connected the return of winter's *Norway* dark days in December with the return of the dead. This made the Christmas season a time of anxiety over crops and weather in the year to come, blended with joy. The Norwegian Christmas today is an interesting combination of Christian customs with quaint practices from the past. The marzipan pig, special Christmas games, and an "elf's porridge" are as traditional as the celebration of Christ's birth.

This is a time for great feasting, frolic, visiting, and singing. Until recent generations trees as well as animals were honored on Christmas Eve with special rations. Today in various parts of Scandinavia it would be more customary to set a bowl of porridge in the hayloft of the barn. This is the family's gift to the "barn elf" whose special domain is the stable and the loft.

Straw is an important symbol in this northern country. In earlier times it was spread over dirt floors and after the Christmas season it was scattered over the land to increase its fertility. Although an insignificant part of present Norwegian customs, straw remains a legendary symbol.

Norwegian housewives, like their Swedish neighbors, are noted for their extensive preparations for the holiday season and for their impressive assortment of holiday breads, cakes, and other specialties. These include *Julekake*, a cakelike citron bread, and *Hjortetaak*, doughnut-like cakes made in an "E" shape. Then there is the stand-by *Flatbrød*, which is made from oat flour and is baked over a slow peat fire. Another is the fruited and seasoned Christmas bread. The recipe listed below is for a kind of *Julekake* and comes from the files of Mrs. Marguerite Ingrim, in Illinois.

JULEKAKE
Norwegian Christmas Bread

    2 cups milk
    1 cup butter or margarine, melted
    2 teaspoons salt
    1 cup sugar
    2 cakes yeast
    ½ cup lukewarm water
    8 cups flour
    1 tablespoon cardamom seeds
    ½ cup chopped almonds
    ½ cup candied cherries, sliced
    ⅔ cup citron, loosely packed and chopped fine
    1 cup chopped raisins

Scald milk and put into large mixing bowl. Add melted butter, salt, and sugar. When lukewarm, stir in yeast which has been dissolved in ½ cup lukewarm water. Stir in 4 cups of the flour, cover with a cloth and put dough in a warm place to rise until double in bulk (about 2 hours). Remove dough and place on floured board; punch down and stir in crushed cardamom seeds, almond meats, and fruits. Work in rest of flour until dough is as soft as can be conveniently handled. Cover and let rise in a warm place (80°–85°) until double in bulk (about 2 hours). Knead slightly and shape into loaves. Place in 2 regular or 3 small greased loaf pans. Let rise until double in bulk. Bake in preheated moderate oven (350°) 50 to 60 minutes, until golden brown. Let cool in pan; then glaze with a thin Confectioners' Sugar Icing (see page 156).

Makes 3 small loaves.

Sweden

There is an old expression that "Christmas lasts a month in Sweden," which is often taken literally. This is not quite true, but the holiday season does commence early with the celebration of *Luciadagen* on December 13 and does not end until January 13, *Tjugondag Knut,* the day dedicated to the martyred Saint Hilary. From Christmas Eve until the new year comes in, emphasis is on family and friends. In modern Sweden, many of the old customs and folklore make the season a real festival of the home with cordial hospitality freely dispensed.

Particularly in the rural sections, preparations for the yule season are begun early in December. Baking becomes a kind of kitchen ceremonial, and a wide variety of breads and buns as well as cakes and cookies of many shapes and colors are made. The breads include sweet and dark wort bread, pungent saffron loaves, gingersnaps in various patterns, and *Lussekatter*—saffron-flavored buns. These Lucia Buns (literally, "Lucia Cats") have a proud heritage for they grew out of the legend of Saint Lucia.

Lucia was born in Syracuse, Sicily, about A.D. 283, of noble family. On the eve of her marriage she gave all of her dowry to the poor of her village and publicly pronounced that she had become a Christian. For this she was accused of being a witch and was sentenced to death

on December 13, A.D. 304. One legend is that before being put to death she was tortured and her eyes removed so that she could no longer attract any man by her beauty.

After her death she was canonized and thus received the name of Saint Lucia. Throughout Italy and Sicily her *festa* of December 13 is celebrated with bonfires, torchlight processions, and illuminations. The Festival of Light in the north has replaced the religious observance of the south.

In Sweden, Saint Lucia's *festa* comes near the time of

the winter solstice, and symbolizes the revival of light as well as a time of peace and prosperity in the fields. Actually the winter solstice occurs on December 22 rather than December 13. The difference in dates is explained by the adoption of the Gregorian calendar, in 1753. Lucia's day is still celebrated on December 13, according to the ancient Julian calendar. The old beliefs are thus deepened through this celebration since the return of light has always been considered a symbol of hope and charity in the traditions of the Swedish people.

Luciadagen is essentially a day of family celebration, and its old-time customs are still practiced in many homes, particularly in remote rural areas. The Swedish ceremony is a pretty one. Up before dawn, the youngest daughter is "Lucia" for a day. She dresses all in white or circles her long white robe with a red band, and with this wears red stockings. She tops her golden tresses with a crown of lingonberries or greens on which nine white candles are lighted. She then serves each member of the family with bedside coffee, saffron bread or buns, and cookies. Often she sings a Christmas song for good measure.

Recently there has been increasing emphasis on a kind of community observance of *Luciadagen* in some of Sweden's larger cities. The community elects a Lucia Queen, as our communities elect beauty queens. She presides over *Luciadagen* events including a parade, often combined with fund raising for charity.

In Stockholm, the queen and her court parade the streets of the gaily decorated capital, riding in carriages brightened with ornamentation. The parade terminates at the City Hall where a banquet is held, the highlight of which is the presentation of the Lucia ornament. Since the awarding of the Nobel Prize takes place on December 10, a Nobel Prize winner is usually on hand to make the presentation to the reigning queen.

In other cities Lucia's court may be composed of a man

on horseback and boys and girls of Lucia's church parish. The girl attendants wear long white gowns for the crowning of the queen and they carry white candles. The boys, known as star boys, also wear white and cover their heads with peaked silver caps decorated with star and moon cutouts. Sometimes Lucia is also attended by baker boys who carry trays of the Lucia Cat buns, made in X shapes with curled ends and raisin eyes. They do not look a bit like cats; they suggest an old-time ceremonial bread, and the X shape might even be interpreted as the Greek letter χ [*Chi*], which stands for Christ.

Lucia and her attendants sing old Christmas songs much as our carolers do in America. But unlike the carolers here, who are offered hospitality as they make their singing calls, Swedish boys and girls offer food wherever they go.

LUSSEKATTER
Lucia Buns

Use Basic Sweet Dough recipe (page 34), adding ½ teaspoon saffron to milk. If you don't care for the bitter-sweet flavor of saffron, substitute about 20 cardamom seeds ground in a mortar or 1 tablespoon ground carda-mom. Cut off a piece of dough and shape into a 15-inch roll. Or cut dough into strips about 5 inches long and ½ inch wide. Place two strips together to form the letter X on a greased baking sheet. Dot with raisins. Cover, set in a warm place (80°–85°) and let rise for about 1 hour, until double in size. Brush with egg-water mixture to glaze. Bake in hot oven (400°) for about 12 minutes.

Or you may roll into long pieces of dough and cut into 10-inch lengths. Form each length into an S-shaped twist and coil up both ends of each twist. Put raisins at both starting points, let rise, glaze, and bake in a moderate oven (375°) about 20 minutes.

Makes 24 to 30 buns.

Or make Vicar's Hair, old-fashioned wig-shaped buns. Divide the dough into three parts and shape each part into a 12-inch roll. Form each roll into a big scallop and proceed as for Lucia Buns.

Bells signal Christmas joy in Switzerland from the *Switzerland* smallest Alpine village to its few teeming cities. The mellow tones of the crooknecked Alpine horns, the tinkle

of cowbells, the gay notes of sleigh bells, and the deep
resounding peal of church bells that send their echoes
through snow-covered valleys and mountain villages, all
are a part of the Christmas season.

Switzerland is essentially a country of small communities so that many of the ancient folk customs remain.
There is no single pattern of observance for customs have
stemmed from the four linguistic groups—German,
French, Italian, and Romanche or Swiss. Here, as in other
countries, the influence of pre-Christian myths regarding
crops and weather remains conspicuous.

In the French and German sections of the country gifts
are brought by the *Christkindli*, the Christ Child. According to popular belief, he represents Christ as a child, and
he is often connected with an angel bearing a light or star,
just as an angel heralded the birth of Christ in Bethlehem.

Candles are frequently used to illuminate Christmas
trees in Switzerland, even though homes are wired for
electricity today. Parents decorate the tree with gay ornaments on Christmas Eve. Candy, fruit, nuts, and cookies
in bright wrappings are also used. Christmas poems are
often read before gifts are distributed, and often the
family gathers about the tree to sing carols as in German
and Austrian homes. In the French-speaking regions gifts
are distributed on New Year's Day.

In mountain areas in particular, everyone dresses up in
his Sunday best and goes to church on Christmas Eve,
sometimes riding through fields covered with snow to
attend the midnight church service.

Special holiday foods vary from region to region and
reflect cultural origins. One that I like very much is the
Swiss Christmas Bread—it is rich and delicious and includes an interesting variety of dried fruits.

WEIHNACHTSBRODT
Swiss Christmas Bread

Madame L. Hertig of Besançon, France, generously shares this recipe from the Switzerland of her childhood.

⅓   cup sliced dried peaches
⅓   cup sliced dried pears
⅓   cup seeded raisins
⅓   cup candied cherries
¼   cup cubed citron
1   teaspoon candied lemon peel, finely cut
½   cup finely cut nutmeats
2   tablespoons brandy or vanilla
½   teaspoon nutmeg
½   teaspoon cinnamon
¼   teaspoon cloves
1   cup milk
¼   cup water
1   cake yeast, or envelope active dry yeast
¼   cup melted butter or margarine
¼   cup sugar
1   teaspoon salt
1   egg, lightly beaten
3½   cups or more flour

Sprinkle the fruits and nuts with the brandy or vanilla and seasonings, and let stand for at least 8 hours or overnight. Heat milk and water to lukewarm and stir in butter, sugar, and salt. If you use compressed yeast, crumble into lukewarm milk and water mixture. If you use active dry yeast, combine with 1 cup flour and other dry ingredients and follow steps outlined in Basic Sweet Dough (page 34), beating in enough flour to make a soft and manageable dough. Pat into shape and put into a large greased bowl, turn the dough over, and cover with damp cloth. Set aside in a warm place (80°–85°) until dough is double in size.

Punch down and turn out onto lightly floured board; knead 5 minutes, until smooth and satiny. Work in the fruit-nut mixture, and divide dough into two parts. Shape into loaves, and put the dough into greased bread pans. Cover and let stand until loaves have almost doubled in size. Brush with melted butter. Bake in preheated moderate (375°) oven 45 minutes, or until a rich golden brown. Let bread stand for 10 minutes, then turn out onto rack to cool. Frost loaves with a topping of Confectioners' Sugar Icing (page 156), adding 1 teaspoon brandy to it if extra flavor is desired.

POTICA
Yugoslavian Christmas Bread

Rich and delicious, this is an excellent choice for a   *Yugoslavia*
morning coffee or an afternoon tea.

Follow directions for Basic Sweet Dough (page 34). After
dough has doubled in size turn it out onto board and
divide into 3 parts. Roll each part into a rectangle of
1/4-inch thickness. Spread the rectangles with the cocoa-
honey filling and roll them up like jelly rolls.

FILLING
½   cup sugar
2   tablespoons softened margarine
2   eggs
2   cups chopped walnut meats
½   cup honey
½   cup cocoa
2   tablespoons milk

Put rolls on oiled baking sheets and let them rise in a
warm place (80°–85°) until doubled in size. Bake in a
preheated moderate oven (350°) 30 to 40 minutes until
well browned. Brush lightly with softened margarine.

Makes 3 long rolled loaves.

OTHER CHRISTMAS BREADS

A Christmas bread which I have found to have excellent
texture and flavor is the bread which is a favorite of Mrs.
Frank Scrogin of Whittier, California, and which she
makes with rolled oats. She makes a double batch of it
for holiday use in order to give a loaf to each of her ten

neighborhood friends "under ten." With the bread Mrs. Scrogin gives each child a big red Washington apple and her holiday good wishes.

Vegetable oil may be substituted for the butter (⅓ cup).

CHRISTMAS RAISIN BREAD

1	medium-sized potato
2	cups hot water
1	cup rolled oats (quick or old-fashioned)
1½	cups seedless raisins
2	teaspoons salt
¼	cup brown sugar, firmly packed
1	tablespoon honey
¼	cup (½ stick) butter or margarine
2	envelopes active dry yeast
½	cup warm water
4½	cups (or more) flour

Peel potato and cut into thick slices. Put into saucepan and cover with hot water then boil until tender. Mash it in saucepan with water in which it was boiled, then add enough hot water to make two cups liquid. Put into large, deep bowl the rolled oats, raisins, salt, brown sugar, honey, and butter. Bring potato liquid to boil again, force through strainer into bowl containing other ingredients. Stir to blend. Let cool to lukewarm, about ½ hour.

Into another bowl put yeast with warm water. Let stand 10 minutes. Combine with potato mixture. Stir thoroughly. To this add 1 cup white flour slowly, stirring as bubbles form. Add another cup and stir, then remaining flour until dough can be handled.

Turn out onto floured board, knead into shape. Sprinkle inside of bowl with flour, put dough in. Cover with a lightly dampened towel and let stand in warm (80°–85°), sheltered place until double in size (1½ to 2 hours). Punch down, pull edges in to center, and turn completely over

in bowl. Let rise again until doubled (30 to 45 minutes).
Turn out onto lightly floured bowl and knead and shape
into six small loaves. Put into six 3 × 5 × 2-inch well-
greased bread pans. Let rise until rounded above pan,
and bake in slow oven (325°) about 50 minutes, until
golden brown. Brush tops sparingly with butter or margarine. Let cool. Then ice tops with frosting, such as Confectioners' Sugar Icing (page 156).

Makes 6 small loaves.

Hanukkah (also spelled Chanukah) is derived from the   *Israel*
Hebrew word meaning dedication. It is also called the
"Feast of Dedication" and the "Festival of Light." It always starts on the twenty-fifth day of the Jewish month
of Kislev. Because the Jewish calendar is based on the
moon, not the sun, the Jewish holidays fall each year on
varying dates of the solar 365-day calendar. Since Hanukkah is usually celebrated in December, it sometimes
coincides with Christmas.

The Festival of Light, one of the most joyous of all
Jewish holidays, commemorates the military and spiritual victory of Judas Maccabaeus and his army over the
king of Syria, who attempted to crush the Jewish faith in
one god, and the rededication of the temple.

Hanukkah is celebrated for eight days by lighting the
candles of the *menorah* (candelabra) which is placed on a
windowsill so that it may be seen by passers-by. The special *menorah* used for Hanukkah holds nine candles, one
for each of the eight days of Hanukkah, and a center
candle which is called the *shamash*, which is used to light
the Hanukkah candles.

At sundown on the first day, the head of the household
lights the first candle while the other members of the
family gather around. A new candle is lit each evening,

moving from right to left to correspond to the direction of Hebrew writing, until on the eighth night eight Hanukkah candles are aflame in addition to the *shamash.*

Special prayers are recited after the lighting of the candles and often a short story is read explaining the celebration. The family sings the hymn *Maoz Tsur,* which is known as the "Rock of Ages" in English (although it is not the same hymn).

Hanukkah is the time of giving gifts to children, spinning the *dreidel,* top, and of serving special delicacies to family and friends. Among them is the famed potato pancake, *Latke,* the number-one traditional favorite. Other specialties may include *Kreplach,* filled noodle-dough triangles, *Strudel,* made of noodle pastry with extra butter and rolled paper-thin before cutting into shapes and adding fillings, *Mandelbrot,* an almond-cinnamon cooky, and *Hamantaschen,* filled triangles. A sesame or poppy-seed flavored yeast bread called *Challah* (pronounced hallah), which is particularly used for Friday night services in the home and is served with wine before the meal and at Purim, is a bread many of us like to make for December use. It is so excellent that I use it many months of the year and especially like it with the addition of colorful and pungent saffron.

When I dip into my precious packet of powdered saffron for December baking my mind goes back to those ancient times when the peoples of the Mediterranean Basin carried the saffron crocus over their trade routes to spreading civilizations. It has been cloaked in romance since the days of Queen Nefertiti, the beautiful wife of Ikhnaton, back in the fourteenth century B.C. Dedicated to the sun, the saffron crocus was cultivated in King Solomon's garden, Cleopatra was said to have blended it in some of her favorite cosmetics, and the Egyptians used it in religious ceremonies.

Seventy-five thousand blossoms of the saffron crocus are

required to produce one pound of saffron powder, making it the most expensive of all spices.

This Jewish egg bread has excellent texture and flavor, particularly with the addition of saffron. Its golden slices are so colorful that I make many loaves for holiday use.

GOLDEN CHALLAH

1   envelope active dry yeast
4½ cups flour
1   tablespoon sugar
2   teaspoons salt
¼   teaspoon powdered saffron
1¼ cups warm water, or ½ cup warm water and ¾ cup milk
2   tablespoons vegetable oil, warmed
2   eggs or 4 egg whites
1   egg yolk, lightly beaten
3   tablespoons sesame seeds

Mix undissolved yeast with one third of the flour, to which sugar and salt have been added. Make a well in the center. Dissolve saffron in ¼ cup warm water, and pour into well. Gradually add remaining warm water and oil. Beat for 2 minutes at medium speed of electric mixer, scraping the bowl as necessary. Add about ½ cup flour to make a thick batter. Drop in eggs and egg yolk, beating 2 minutes more at high speed. Stir in remaining flour to

make a soft and manageable dough. Form into a ball and turn onto a lightly floured board. Knead until smooth and elastic. Form into a ball and place in a large bowl lightly oiled. Turn so that oiled side is on top, cover and set in a warm place (80°–85°) to rise. When double in bulk (about 1 hour), turn dough onto board and punch down. Divide dough in half. Form half the dough into a 12-inch roll, and cut into six equal parts. Between lightly floured hands, roll the dough into six ropes of equal length. Braid three ropes together, pressing the beginning ends tightly to hold. Repeat with second three ropes. Place the braided loaves on an oiled cooky sheet. Cover and let rise once more until almost double in bulk. Then brush braided tops with beaten egg yolk combined with 1 tablespoon water; sprinkle with sesame seeds. Let rise, uncovered, in a warm place (80°–85°) until doubled in bulk (about 1 hour). Bake in a preheated moderate (375°) oven for 40 to 50 minutes, until golden brown. Remove from cooky sheet and let cool on wire racks.

Makes 2 loaves.

In Argentina, as in other Catholic countries, Christmas is observed as a religious and family celebration. Midnight Mass, also called "Cock's Mass" here, attracts all Catholics. Aside from the religious observance of the Nativity, the Christmas season is generally a time of joy and merriment; on Christmas Eve firecrackers are shot off in the streets, lighting up the sky in a rainbow of colors. After the Cock's Mass, dried fruits, hazelnuts, walnuts, almonds, cider, and cocoa are served to the children. *Pan Dulce* is featured at this time, according to our friend Mr. Antonio Amici of Pergamino, Argentina.

On Christmas Day the main meal or dinner is served at noon. Turkey is not as available as in the United States and in Argentina the menu features ravioli, spaghetti, baked pork, chicken, salads, and fresh fruit. But of course the national specialty is *Empanadas,* small meat pies (page 232).

Desserts consist of fruit salads—to counteract the heat of December days and nights—cakes, and *pasteles.* Though *pasteles* may be loosely translated as "pies," they are more like our George Washington Pie and the Boston Cream Pie, which are actually cakes. The Argentine *pastele* is formed of two layers of pastry containing a piece of jam —in Argentina jam is made in solid form and can be cut in pieces. The favored jam is made of sweet potatoes. The corners of the layers are folded in a special shape, then the *pastele* is deep-fried in oil. Since they are small, the Argentine housewife makes dozens of these delicacies at a time.

Families often gather in the garden, for Christmas in Argentina is in summer and it is often warm on Christmas Eve. The tree is trimmed with colored paper garlands encircling it and flowers made of paper hung upon it. Near its base or at one side is the crib that holds a doll that represents the Infant Jesus. Music is in the air as *villancicos,* Christmas carols, are sung by old and young. Every region has its own traditional *villancicos,* but all of them stress the joy of the Savior's birth, the sadness of his known destiny and sufferings, according to our friend Mr. Rafael Silberman of Santa Rosa, Argentina.

Christmas Eve is the most important single celebration of the year in this South American country, and a memorable one for its religious observance, pageantry, joyous music, and special Christmas foods. The Christmas Eve dinner following midnight Mass is the festive meal but delicacies are served throughout the festival period and *Pan Dulce* is a "must" for Christmas breakfast.

The recipe for *Pan Dulce,* a delicious Argentine fruit bread, comes to us though the courtesy of Mr. Rafael Silberman.

QUICK BREADS

PAN DULCE
Argentine Quick Bread

1 cup shortening
¾ cup sugar
3 eggs, lightly beaten
1 cup self-rising flour
½ cup milk (if necessary)
¼ cup candied orange peel, chopped
¼ cup candied cherries, chopped
¼ cup raisins
2 teaspoons vanilla

Mix shortening and sugar. Add beaten eggs. Add flour alternately with milk. Blend in chopped candied fruits, raisins, and vanilla. Grease and flour a bread pan about 12 × 4 × 5 inches deep. Bake in preheated moderate oven (350°) about 1 hour and 20 minutes.

Makes 1 loaf.

Christmas comes in Chile at the hottest part of the year when many people are on vacation. *Viejo Pascuero,* as Santa Claus is called in this South American country, travels through the sky with his reindeer and enters each home through an open window. Children learn that he will not visit their home unless they are asleep, but like children everywhere they beg to be allowed to stay awake just to get a peek at him. Parents do not relent, any more than they do elsewhere, and Christmas morning children awaken to find that *Viejo Pascuero* has come and gone, leaving gifts behind him.

In many parts of Chile a special bread is served at breakfast on Christmas morning, and *Azuela de Ave* (chicken soup made with potatoes, onions, and corn on the cob) is featured at the festive dinner. A long-handled fork is used for spearing and eating the corn.

The round Christmas breakfast loaf of bread is filled with candied fruit and is leavened either with yeast or with baking powder. The yeast-leavened loaf is rather complicated to make and is usually bought by Chilean housewives these days, so I will share the quicker-to-make, rich-flavored *Pan de Pascua,* as given me by Nancy Dick of Santiago. I am indebted to her and to my cousin Barbara Smith Maginnis, who spent two years in Copiapo, Chile, with the Peace Corps, for background information on Chilean customs and foods.

PAN DE PASCUA
Chilean Christmas Bread

1   cup butter (2 sticks)
1   tablespoon margarine

2   cups sugar
5   eggs, separated
1   cup seeded raisins
1   cup candied mixed fruit peel
2   tablespoons brandy or rum
5   cups flour (or more)
2   tablespoons baking powder
1½   cups milk
1   cup chopped nutmeats
1   tablespoon powdered anise

Cream butter, margarine, and sugar. Then add the egg yolks one by one, beating after each addition. Meanwhile put fruits in the brandy or rum and let stand. To the butter-sugar mixture add the combined flour and baking powder alternately with the milk. Then add the nuts, anise, fruit mixture, and lastly the egg whites, well beaten. Pour into greased casserole dishes or into two long 12 × 4 × 5-inch bread pans. Bake in moderate oven (375°) for 15 minutes, then lower to 350° and bake about 45 minutes until golden brown.

Makes 2 loaves.

Ireland   *The Margaret Rudkin Pepperidge Farm Cookbook* said that tea in Ireland is not just a simple cup of tea and a biscuit. Served at the dining-room table, the usual tea, holiday time or not, begins with slices of brown Irish Soda Bread and slices of white bread thickly buttered, with accompanying jams, "hot crusty scones, a plate of cookies, a 'sponge sandwich' cake (two layers of sponge cake, jam between and sugar sprinkled on top), and a chocolate cake with thick, creamy chocolate icing—or warm gingerbread cake full of currants." With this sumptuous spread, three or four cups of tea for each guest are served. Special-occasion teas may feature bowls of fruit,

such as fresh raspberries or strawberries topped with whipped cream, or bottled fruit which has been kept in the cool larder.

This took me back in memory to my childhood days and my Grandmother Palmer, who had a "touch" of Irish in her and made brown Irish Soda Bread all of the years that I can remember her baking in her wood range, heated with oak logs about 14 inches in length. In the old-fashioned way, Friday was baking day. And Grandma reasoned that if soda bread was a good bread for spring, summer, and fall, it was a good bread for winter and for December too.

Many cooks may choose to make the Irish *Barmbrack*, a yeast bread rich with currants, cherries, raisins, and cinnamon, and with better keeping qualities than Soda Bread. For my part, I will stay with the fine old brown Irish Soda Bread of my childhood for some of my Christmas use.

GRANDMA'S IRISH SODA BREAD

1½ cups unsifted whole-wheat flour
½   cup high-protein white flour
1   teaspoon salt
1   teaspoon soda
½   teaspoon cream of tartar
1   tablespoon melted shortening
¼   cup unsulfured molasses
¾   cup sour milk

Mix flours, salt, soda, and cream of tartar in a large mixing bowl. Make a well in the center, and add shortening, molasses, and sour milk. Mix together to form a dough, adjusting quantity of sour milk as necessary. Pat into a ball, and turn out onto a lightly floured board. Knead 5 minutes. Shape into a circular loaf and place in a lightly greased 2-quart casserole or baking dish. Bake in a preheated moderate oven (375°) about 1 hour. (If you use a glass baking dish, test for doneness at 45 minutes.)
Makes 1 loaf.

Another bread that requires no kneading comes from Dr. Helen Christensen's kitchen and brings enthusiastic appreciation in December or any time of the year it is served. Delicious plain, it is also excellent toasted or served with slices of assorted cheeses.

CASSEROLE DISH BATTER BREAD

¼   cup margarine
¼   cup brown sugar
2   teaspoons salt
1   cup milk

1   cup warm water
2   envelopes active dry yeast
3   cups flour
2   cups rye flour
2   tablespoons caraway seeds

Heat margarine with sugar, salt, milk, and water.
Add yeast to flours and combine with milk mixture in a
large bowl, stirring after each addition until all is used
and well mixed. Put in a veɪy large greased bowl, and
cover with a damp cloth. Let rise in a warm place
(80°–85°) until almost double in bulk (about 1 to 1½
hours). Stir batter down and place in a well-greased 2- to
3-quart round casserole. Let rise again until almost
double in size. Brush tops with milk and a sprinkling of
caraway seeds. Bake in a moderate oven (350°) for about
45 minutes, until brown.
    Note: Water and powdered milk may be substituted
for milk.
    Makes 1 or more round loaves.

BANANA NUT BREAD

1   cup light brown sugar, firmly packed
½   cup margarine
2   eggs
1½   cups mashed banana (3 to 4 bananas)
1   tablespoon lemon juice
2   cups sifted flour
3   teaspoons baking powder
½   teaspoon salt
1   cup chopped nutmeats

Cream sugar with margarine. Add eggs, one at a time,
beating hard after each addition. Stir in bananas and
lemon juice. Sift together flour, baking powder, and salt;
add and mix quickly. Stir in nuts. Pour into greased
9 × 5 × 3-inch loaf pan. Bake in moderate oven (350°)

for 1 hour, or until it tests done (when a toothpick is inserted in center and comes out dry).

Makes 1 loaf.

CRANBERRY NUT BREAD

2   cups sifted flour
¾   cup granulated sugar
3   teaspoons baking powder
1   teaspoon salt
½   teaspoon soda
1   teaspoon cinnamon
1   cup chopped walnuts
1   egg
1   cup whole cranberry sauce, drained
2   tablespoons vegetable oil

Sift together onto waxed paper the flour, sugar, baking powder, salt, soda, and cinnamon. Add walnuts. In mixing bowl, beat egg; add cranberry sauce and shortening. Add dry ingredients. Stir until just blended. Pour into greased 9 × 5 × 3-inch loaf pan. Bake in moderate oven (350°) 55 minutes. Cool on rack.

Makes 1 loaf.

Note: 1 teaspoon grated lemon rind may also be added. Use ½ cup cranberry sauce remaining in can to blend with 1 3-ounce package cream cheese as a spread for tea sandwiches.

JIFFY ORANGE CRANBERRY BREAD

1   14-ounce package orange muffin mix
1   egg
1   cup cranberry orange relish

Blend orange muffin mix with egg and cranberry orange relish. Stir until just blended (mixture will be slightly lumpy). Pour mixture into $8\frac{1}{2} \times 4\frac{1}{2} \times 3$ or a $9 \times 5 \times 3$-inch loaf pan. Bake in preheated moderate oven (350°) for 45 to 50 minutes, until toothpick inserted comes out clean and crust is golden brown.

Makes 1 loaf.

MINCEMEAT BREAD

This quick bread is pleasantly rich, makes use of packaged mincemeat, and slices well for cheese or other spread for holiday use.

1   9-ounce package mincemeat
½   cup cold water
¼   cup margarine
½   cup sugar
1   egg, lightly beaten
½   cup chopped walnut meats
2½   cups sifted flour
1   tablespoon double-acting baking powder
½   teaspoon salt

Break up package of mincemeat into small pieces. Place with cold water in a small saucepan and stir over low heat until mixture becomes smooth; then boil until almost dry, stirring constantly to avoid scorching. Cool thoroughly. Cream margarine; add sugar and continue to cream. Add beaten egg. Continue to beat until well blended. Stir in the cold mincemeat mixture alternately with nutmeats.

Combine flour, baking powder, and salt. Sift twice, then add alternately with milk to first mixture, blending well after each addition. Pour dough into greased 9 × 5 × 3-inch loaf pan, being sure that sides of batter are higher than the center. Bake in a preheated moderate oven (350°) for about 70 minutes until done. Remove from oven; let stand 10 minutes, then invert on wire rack to cool. For best results, make at least a day before use. Slice very thin and spread with butter, margarine, cream cheese, or jelly (plum is particularly good).

Makes 1 loaf.

ORANGE NUT BREAD

2   cups sifted flour
2   teaspoons baking powder
½   cup sugar
½   teaspoon salt
1   cup raisins
½   cup chopped nutmeats
¼   cup grated orange peel
¾   cup sliced pitted dates
1   beaten egg
¼   cup orange juice
2   tablespoons vegetable oil
½   teaspoon baking soda

Sift flour, baking powder, sugar, and salt. Add raisins, nutmeats, orange peel, and dates, and mix. Combine egg, orange juice, and vegetable oil and add to flour-fruit mixture. Stir to mix thoroughly. Add soda and blend, preferably in mixer about 1 minute at medium speed. Pour batter into a greased 10 × 3½ × 2¾-inch pan. Bake in a preheated moderate oven about 60 minutes.

Makes 1 large loaf.

This is an excellent nut bread recipe for general use and for anyone who must restrict saturated fat in his diet.

PEPPAR KOEK
Dutch Teacake

Mrs. A. H. van Diggelen vouches for the authenticity of this old, rich-scented teacake which she has baked successfully for many years in her Piedmont, California, kitchen. She slices *Peppar Koek* very thin and serves it as we would a nut-enriched bread.

4   cups flour
2   teaspoons baking powder
1   cup light brown sugar
1   cup molasses (Brer Rabbit, Green Label)
1   cup mixed candied fruit peels, including some citron
1   teaspoon cinnamon
½   teaspoon cloves
1   cup (¼ pint) milk

Sift dry ingredients together and mix in other ingredients. Pour into two greased 9 × 5 × 3-inch bread pans and bake in slow oven (300°) about 2 hours.

Makes 2 loaves.

We are more accustomed to the delicate nutlike flavor of sesame seeds in cakes and coffeecakes, but sesame is widely used in the Far East and in Sicily as an ingredient of bread. Sesame has been grown in the Near East, Far East, and Africa for many centuries. It was well known in Old Testament times and was an important food in the days of Cleopatra, for its very high protein content. Sesame lacks the aromatic qualities of many spices but its seeds are crunchy and nutlike and are used in many Christmas recipes for fillings for coffeecake and as a topping for breads and cakes. When toasted, sesame seeds are valuable additions to many other dishes. They can be toasted in a moderate oven (350°) for five minutes in a lightly oiled baking dish.

One delicious use of sesame seeds is in Persian Quick Bread. A round, flat loaf, Persian Quick Bread is good cut in wedges and spread with butter or cream cheese.

PERSIAN QUICK BREAD

3   cups flour
1   tablespoon baking powder
1   teaspoon salt
4   tablespoons margarine
⅔   cup milk
1   egg, slightly beaten
3   scant tablespoons toasted sesame seeds

To the flour add baking powder and salt, and sift twice together into mixing bowl. Cut margarine into flour mixture with pastry blender. With a knife blade stir in the milk and egg and stir to blend in dry mixture, but not to make a smooth dough. Dough will be sticky to touch. Turn onto a floured board and sprinkle lightly with flour, then knead ten times. Pat but do not roll dough into oiled layer cake pan, covering entire surface. Sprinkle top with sesame seeds, and bake in a hot oven (400°) about 35 minutes, until golden brown and done. Let cool on a wire rack and cut into wedges. Serve cold.

Makes 1 loaf—12 servings.

PUMPKIN BREAD

The use of pumpkin dates to our Pilgrim forebears, and Pumpkin Bread is a real conversation piece with its rich color and zestful flavor. It is a fine addition to a sandwich tray when spread with cream cheese, unusual enough to feature at a coffee or tea. It came to me many years ago from Mabel Wayland of Del Monte, California.

2⅔ cups sugar
⅔ cup vegetable oil
1 teaspoon cloves
½ teaspoon nutmeg
2 cups canned pumpkin
1 teaspoon soda
½ teaspoon baking powder
4 eggs
1¼ teaspoons salt
1 teaspoon cinnamon
⅔ cup hot water
3⅓ cups flour
1 cup nutmeats, chopped fine

Put all ingredients except nuts into large mixing bowl. Beat to blend. Add nutmeats and mix thoroughly. Pour into greased 1-pound cans, filling the cans about three-fourths full; or use 9 × 5 × 3-inch loaf pans. Bake in moderate oven (350°) 40 to 60 minutes. Test with tooth-pick for doneness. Loaves can be frozen for later use.

Makes 4 small loaves.

APPLE BISCUITS

These biscuits, served in many old plantation homes of the Deep South, were leavened with yeast and would have been made about like this:

- 1 tablespoon butter
- 1 cup scalded milk
- 1 tablespoon sugar
- ½ cake yeast
- ¼ cup warm water
- ½ teaspoon salt
- 2 cups flour
- 1 cup pared, grated apple
- ½ teaspoon soda
  - Butter
  - Cinnamon

Melt butter (margarine may be substituted) in hot milk, and add sugar. Cool to warm. Dissolve yeast in ¼ cup warm water and stir in warm milk mixture. Sift together salt and 1 cup flour. Make a well in center and pour in liquid. Beat vigorously. Pour into a greased bowl, turn once so top is greased, cover with a dampened cloth, and let rise in a warm place (80°–85°).

Grate pared apple into batter and mix carefully to blend. Sift together soda with remaining cup of flour, and add to batter. Stir thoroughly. Work into a ball and turn into greased bowl. Cover (with a dampened cloth) and let rise until double in size (about 1 hour). Shape into round cakes with hand. Let stand for about 15 minutes until light. Bake in a preheated hot oven (400°) 12 to 15 minutes, until browned. Butter the tops and sprinkle with cinnamon.

Makes about 20 biscuits.

SPICY CRANBERRY MUFFINS
(Courtesy of Ocean Spray Cranberry Kitchen)

1   cup cranberry orange relish
¼   cup light brown sugar
1   tablespoon flour
½   cup chopped pecans
2   cups biscuit mix
3   tablespoons sugar
1   teaspoon cinnamon
¼   teaspoon nutmeg
1   egg
¾   cup milk

Topping: Combine cranberry orange relish, brown sugar, flour, and pecans. Spoon 1 tablespoon of mixture into each of 12 greased muffin pan cups.

Muffins: Stir together biscuit mix, sugar, cinnamon, and nutmeg. Stir together egg and milk. Add to dry ingredients stirring just to moisten. Fill muffin cups ⅔ full.

Bake in preheated hot oven (400°) 15 to 20 minutes. Remove from oven and invert pan immediately.

Makes 12 muffins.

MINCEMEAT MUFFINS

1   beaten egg
½   cup moist mincemeat
½   cup apple juice
1   14-ounce package oatmeal muffin mix
1   teaspoon grated orange peel
1   cup confectioners' sugar
4   teaspoons milk
½   teaspoon rum extract

Combine egg, mincemeat, and apple juice in mixing bowl. Add the muffin mix and orange peel all at once. Stir just until blended. Pour into greased 12-muffin pan, filling the cups half full. Bake in preheated hot oven (400°) about 15 minutes or until golden brown. Remove from pan immediately. Blend the confectioners' sugar with milk and rum extract; drizzle over warm muffins.

Makes 12 muffins.

Crisp, toast-brown popovers filled with creamed chicken, turkey, ham, or dried beef are great favorites at our house for December entertaining. Unfilled, they are good with jam at any meal.

My recipe is an old traditional one, but Mama taught me two principles that she thought imperative for "popping" popovers:

1. You must have at least 1⅓ cups of liquid, including eggs, for each cupful of flour. Add an extra egg (or two egg whites) if necessary to get this proportion.

2. Beating should be vigorous.

I will add an observation of my own. To make foolproof popovers, have ingredients at room temperature, mix the ingredients according to directions, and bake at the right temperature. Beat 2 minutes by hand, 1 minute if you use an electric beater.

It does not matter whether we use an iron pan, metal pan, or custard cup for our popovers, and the baking containers need not be preheated as in our mothers' time. A 375° oven is recommended for the entire baking period, but I have known some cooks to get excellent results with hotter ovens—425° or more. If you like a very dry center to your popovers, puncture each popover in two or three places 5 minutes before the end of baking time to let out steam. With these simple guides, even a young cook can win acclaim for her popovers.

POPOVERS

2 eggs, lightly beaten
1 cup milk
1 cup sifted flour
½ teaspoon salt
2 teaspoons melted butter or vegetable oil

Put eggs into mixing bowl and add other ingredients. Beat 2 minutes by hand or 1 minute with electric mixer at medium speed. Pour batter into well oiled, slightly heated popover pans. Bake in a preheated moderate oven (375°) 50 to 60 minutes, or hot oven (425°) for 40 minutes, or until there are no beads of moisture on crust. Do not open oven door until 5 minutes before time specified for baking. Popovers are done when toothpick comes out dry. When done remove at once from pans. Makes 6 to 8 popovers.

TWO QUICK COFFEECAKES

CHRISTMAS RING COFFEECAKE

2   cups biscuit mix
¾   cup milk
⅓   cup margarine
3   tablespoons brown sugar
12 maraschino cherries
¼   cup chopped hazelnuts
    Cinnamon-Sugar

Mix biscuit mix and milk. Shape dough into 12 balls. Melt margarine. Pour half of margarine into a 9-inch ring mold. Add brown sugar, cherries, and nuts. Roll biscuits in other half of melted margarine, place in ring mold, and sprinkle with cinnamon-sugar. Bake in preheated hot oven (400°) for 25 to 30 minutes. Remove from pan while warm. This may also be made in the form of a Christmas tree.
Makes one 9-inch ring.

CRANBERRY COFFEECAKE

Like many coffeecakes, this is good from the first day but improves if allowed to age. I often make and bake it a week ahead of use, freeze, and reheat as needed.

2   tablespoons cranberry sauce
1½ cups milk
2   cups flour
1   teaspoon soda
2   cups sugar
1   teaspoon cinnamon
1   teaspoon cloves

Mix cranberry sauce and milk. Sift flour with soda. Mix all ingredients together and pour into lightly oiled and floured 9-inch-square baking pan. Bake in preheated moderate oven (375°) about 35 minutes, until wooden pick thrust in center comes out clean. Serve warm fresh from oven or store for later use.

Makes one 9-inch-square coffeecake.

OF SUGAR AND SPICE

DECEMBER is a wonderful month for anyone who loves to cook. For it is a special feast time for the sense of smell as well as for the senses of taste and sight. From the moment you check your spice supply until the last cooky is cooled and stored for later use, the bouquets of fragrance are as tantalizing as the most exotic perfume.

Checking of spices is important—experienced cooks are very careful to use only "fresh" spices, herbs, and seasonings for maximum flavor results. In preparation for December baking my own rule of thumb is to discard any ground spice more than six months old. The flavor of almost every spice is diminished by excessive heat or moisture or prolonged exposure to air. Tops that can be kept tightly closed when the spices are not being used help to seal in flavor. Combination dredge and sifter tops are practical because they permit the use of a measuring spoon or the sifting of the spice direct from the container.

Most of us depend upon commercially prepared whole and ground spices and herbs, but some people are lucky enough to have their own herb garden, and can experiment until they know what they like to use and how much spicing they prefer in various recipes. A general guide, however, is to use about twice as much of the fresh seasoning as the dry pulverized form, and to underflavor rather than overflavor.

One of my pleasures, when I sniff the twenty or so spices I use every December, is knowing their histories. Their stories in one sense are an account of Western civilization, for one explorer after another set out to find spices and flavors of the East that would mean commercial profit. There was a time when spices were so precious that wars were fought over them. They were also the basis of earliest trade and commerce.

Peoples of the ancient world sold ointments and oils for large sums of money to the well-to-do ruling classes, who wanted soothing potions and sweet scents to fill their homes. Since the days of the Wise Men and the gifts of frankincense and myrrh to the Christ Child, people have associated fragrant spices with the celebration of His natal day.

Most spices that we accept as commonplace now were indigenous to China—especially the earliest ones. The Arabs transported them by camel caravans over dangerous and treacherous land routes. In this trade the Arabs grew rich and for centuries held tight control of their rewarding monopoly.

If the Arabs had any rivals they were the Phoenicians, who were famed as navigators and men of trade. At Tyre, their richest port, the Bible tells us that they traded "of all spices as well as with precious stones and gold." It is believed that wise and rich King Solomon made some of his great wealth from spices about 1000 B.C., for he built the ships in which the Phoenicians and Israelites went in search of coveted flavors. When the Queen of Sheba visited Solomon, she brought him "a hundred and twenty talents of gold, and of spices of great store."

The Crusades brought men from the East and the West together gastronomically as well as in other ways. European appetites quickened to Eastern flavors. To satisfy this European demand for exotic seasonings from the East, merchant fleets began plying the blue waters of the Mediterranean, carrying spices to the large seaports along the southern coast of Europe.

Venice, the bright cluster of small islands at the head of the Adriatic Sea, had been founded as a buffer against the depredations of the barbarians from the north. With a big merchant fleet backed up by her mighty ships of war, she kept control of all commerce in western waters. She snatched the monopoly on spices from the Arabs as her magnificent port bulged with precious cargoes from the East. From Venice they were consigned by land or by sea to cities having the gold to pay the huge prices charged for the coveted spices. By the late 1400s a pound of cloves was worth two cows in England. Pepper cost forty times its original worth by the time it reached Portugal. Fantastic prices were paid for spices because diets were generally coarse and monotonous by our standards. And food spoiled quickly. Spices served a dual purpose: they disguised unpalatable food flavors and also acted as an anti-oxidant to inhibit spoilage, particularly of meats. Is it any wonder this commerce was so important to the ancients!

   Nation was pitted against nation to discover the best
routes for this lucrative trade. The explorations of Vasco
da Gama, the Polo family, Christopher Columbus, and
Magellan are the tales of intrepid men who set out on long
journeys in poorly equipped ships in quest of the treasures
of spices. Because of the uncertainty of navigation, crews
were reluctant to sign on for such perilous voyages and
often had to be indentured from prisons. It was Marco
Polo who at last unlocked the secret and helped to break
the spice monopoly held so long by the Arabs. Between
1271 and 1295 he traveled extensively through the Near
East, central and southern Asia, and many of the then unknown island chains in the Pacific. On his return he published an account of his three trips to the Orient. He

told of seeing ginger growing in China, cinnamon in Ceylon, pepper in Borneo. Furthermore he had returned part way by sea, indicating a possible passage.

About 1318 Venice and Genoa opened up direct communication by sea with the cities of the Netherlands. Their fleets touched at the port of Lisbon and aroused the interest of the Portuguese in the commerce. Soon they commenced extended maritime expeditions.

On and on it went. The struggle for control of the spice trade widened and deepened with Italy, Portugal, the Netherlands, and England as the contenders. Ships were often clumsy but men in western Europe and later in colonial America found the lure of gold stronger than assurance of safety. Some made fortunes from the sale of spices as trade routes were discovered and charted. Elias Haskett Derby, America's first millionaire, made much of his fortune in pepper. From every harbor of New England's coast hundreds of little schooners, sloops, and brigs put forth each year for distant ports in search of riches to bring back to the homeland. From 1788 to about 1873 almost a thousand "pepper voyages" were made from America's shorelines in search of Sumatra's pepper.

Today hundreds of ships dock at United States ports every year with cargoes of spices, herbs, and seasonings. Within the berry of the pepper, the almond shape of the sesame seed, and the pea-shaped pod that encloses cardamom seeds are treasures that have written some of the story of mankind.

Such a suggestion may send you to your history books. Not until after Christmas, please! Now it is time to be creative with a parade of flavors to enhance your December baking. And remember that it takes time for spices to do their best work for you. Give your Christmas baked specialties time to mellow—to absorb the release of the oils from spices used.

Knowingly used, spices can give an otherwise simple

dish a gourmet quality—but do not overdo. As Irma Mazza writes in *Herbs for the Kitchen,* "He who learns to season truly cooks. But to cook without cunning seasoning is to be only a stoker."

Some Favorite Cakes and Tortes

AMNON once said to the king in II Samuel 13:6, "Let [her] . . . make a couple of cakes in my sight." Amnon referred to a sweetened, sometimes spiced dough that was kneaded a second time to give it lightness. The finished product was a very distant relative to our present cakes, which are as smooth as velvet, soft and crumbly to the touch, moist and beautiful to look at, and delicious to taste. Cake in the days of the Old Testament "tasted like oil" and was a flattened slab of dough baked in the sun.

Marian Maeve O'Brien points out in *The Bible Cookbook* that whether cake was crude or not by our standards, homemakers of those days did indeed make a product that was distinct from bread.

Sometime, somewhere, someone gave me the cake recipe which follows, taken from biblical verses. It seems so appropriate for Christmas use that I include it, and express my thanks to the unknown donor. The key word in each verse appears in italics.

BIBLE CAKE

1	cup	Jeremiah 6:20 "To what purpose cometh there to me incense from Sheba, and the *sweet cane* from a far country? . . ."
½	cup	Judges 5:25 ". . . she brought forth **butter** in a lordly dish."
¾	cup	Judges 4:19 "And she opened a bottle of **milk,** and gave him drink, and covered him."
2	cups	I Kings 4:22 "And Solomon's provision for one day was thirty measures of *fine flour* . . ."
1	tablespoon	I Samuel 14:25 "And all they of the land came to a wood; and there was **honey** upon the ground."

2 teaspoons	Amos 4:5 "And offer a sacrifice of thanksgiving with *leaven*, and proclaim and publish the free offerings . . ."
Season to taste	II Chronicles 9:9 "And she gave the king an hundred and twenty talents of gold, and of *spices* great abundance . . ."
3	Jeremiah 17:11 "As the partridge sitteth on *eggs*, and hatcheth them not; so he that getteth riches, and not by right, shall leave them in the midst of his days, and at his end shall be a fool."
A pinch of	Leviticus 2:13 "And every oblation of thy meat offering shalt thou season with *salt*; neither shalt thou suffer the salt of the covenant of thy God to be lacking from thy meat offering: with all thine offerings thou shalt offer salt."

Rearranged in the order of use, the ingredients would appear as follows, and would give us a very good spiced gold cake.

1 cup vanilla-scented sugar
½ cup butter or margarine
3 eggs, separated
2 cups sifted cake flour
2 teaspoons double-acting baking powder
1 teaspoon cinnamon
½ teaspoon grated nutmeg
¼ teaspoon or more cloves
¼ teaspoon salt
¾ cup milk
1 tablespoon honey

Measure out 1 cup of sugar and store overnight or longer in a tightly closed jar with a vanilla bean. Add scented sugar gradually to softened butter or margarine. Blend until mixture is light and fluffy and lemony in color. Beat in 3 well-beaten egg yolks, setting aside whites for frosting or other use. Resift cake flour (having measured it after first sifting) with baking powder, spices, and salt, adding to the butter mixture in three parts with thirds of ¾ cup milk. Beat the batter until it is smooth after making each addition. Pour into a lightly oiled 9-inch tube pan and bake in a moderate oven (375°) about 45 minutes or until a toothpick inserted in the center comes out clean. Remove from oven and invert to cool. Then add a glaze, jam topping, a sprinkling of confectioners' sugar, or Winter White Frosting (page 160).

Makes one 9-inch cake.

In most countries the Christmas cakes which were baked on the eve of a feast and eaten throughout the time of celebrating were said to bring special blessings of health and good luck. There was a time in the British Isles when a cake was baked on Christmas Eve for every member of the family. Usually these were round cakes flavored with caraway seeds. If a cake happened to break it was a sign of approaching bad luck. Now we associate fruitcake, poundcake, mince pie, and plum pudding with the English Christmas.

The Irish people have a Gaelic name for December 24, *Oidhche na ceapairi*, which means "Night of Cakes."

In Germany and France, Christmas cakes were of great importance. Many of them were elaborately decorated with crystallized sugar figures of the Christ Child. Of the eight basic doughs used in French confectionery, *feuilletage*, flaky pastry, *Pâte Sucrée*, sweet pastry, *Pâte à Savarin*, a yeast-leavened dough, *Génoise*, and *chou* pastry are usually favored for special cakes. Of course almond paste, French pastry cream, *crème pâtissière,* and other creams may be added to the basic doughs to give them the special characteristic required.

France considers its symbolic cakes of great importance, although they are seldom made at home these days. Homemakers buy them at the *pâtisserie.* One such cake is the *Galette des Rois* which, like England's Twelfth Night Cake, is eaten on Epiphany and symbolizes that great feast ritual.

Spain tends to follow the religious pattern of France

and Italy. A familiar Christmas pastry used for family gatherings is *Dulces de almendra.* This is made of sugar, flour, egg whites, and almonds.

Greek Christmas cakes often feature a cross on top as on *Ayio Vassilopitta,* New Year's Cake. In early times, and perhaps even now in a few remote villages, cake was always left on the table on Holy Night in the hope that Christ would stop at the home and eat it. Gifts were not exchanged until January 1, which is the feast day of Saint Basil.

New Year's Eve is a very important family holiday in Greece when even very young children are allowed to stay up to welcome in the New Year. The traditional cake of this celebration is *Ayio Vassilopitta,* which is made of raised yeast dough flavored with lemon or the unusual

Syrian spice called *mah tepi,* which comes from the kernels of black cherries.

A gold or silver coin is wrapped in moistened paper and placed in the dough before it is baked. As the bells chime in the New Year, the head of the family cuts the cake. The recipient of the coin is assured of good luck in the year just born.

AYIO VASSILOPITTA
Greek New Year's Cake

This traditional holiday cake is made by every housewife and usually baked by the village baker.

        1   cake yeast
        1   teaspoon sugar
        ½   cup warm milk
        1   cup milk
        ⅓   cup plus 1 tablespoon margarine
        ¼   cup sugar
        1   teaspoon salt
        ½   teaspoon nutmeg
        ½   teaspoon cinnamon
        2   eggs
        2½   cups flour (approximately)
        ¼   cup chopped, blanched almonds

Dissolve the yeast cake and sugar in ½ cup warm milk. Let stand to form bubbles. Combine remaining milk and margarine in a pan and bring to a boil over low heat. Stir in the ¼ cup sugar, add salt, and pour into a large mixing bowl to cool to lukewarm. Add the nutmeg and cinnamon. Stir in the unbeaten eggs and the yeast mixture. Work in the flour, first with a mixing spoon, later by hand so that dough is thick but not dry. Cover the dough with a damp towel and let stand in a warm place to rise for about an hour. Punch down and knead lightly, and place in a greased cake pan. Insert a well-washed silver coin in the dough. Brush the top with margarine and let rise until double in size. Shape into a flattened ball. Brush the surface with an egg white. Sprinkle with chopped almonds. Bake on a cooky sheet in a moderate oven (350°) for 45 minutes or until it tests done. Turn onto a rack to cool. Then make a cross of Butter Cream Frosting (page 155) on the top.

Makes 1 cake.

CARDAMOM DATE CAKE

Vannee Thokolsri of Bangkok, Thailand, introduced me to the use of many spices native to the Far East which are used extensively in Eastern cookery. One of the favorites is cardamom, and it certainly gives this loaf cake an aromatic flavor.

    1   cup sugar
    ½   cup melted butter or margarine
    2   eggs, well beaten
    4   egg whites, beaten with whole eggs
    4   cups sifted cake flour
    ¼   teaspoon salt
    4   teaspoons baking powder
    ½   cup milk
    1½ cups chopped pitted dates
    1½ cups mixed candied fruits, cut small
    ½   teaspoon or more ground cardamom

In a large mixing bowl combine sugar, butter, and eggs. Beat until smooth. Sift together flour, salt, and baking powder. Add alternately with milk to sugar mixture. Add dates, candied fruit, and cardamom. Fold in carefully and blend. Pour batter into two oiled 9 × 5 × 3-inch loaf pans lined with heavy waxed paper, allowing paper to project on long sides for easy removal. Bake in a slow oven (325°) for one hour or until done.

Makes 2 loaf cakes.

DUNDEE CAKE

This Scottish fruitcake is famous for its almonds which crust the top and for the velvety texture of the cake, rich with assorted candied fruits.

- 2¼ cups sifted cake flour
- 1 teaspoon double-acting baking powder
- ¼ teaspoon salt
- ½ teaspoon ground nutmeg
- ½ teaspoon cinnamon
- ¾ cup margarine
- 1¼ cups sifted confectioners' sugar
- 4 eggs or 2 eggs and 4 egg whites
- ½ cup orange juice
- ½ cup blanched seeded raisins
- ½ cup seedless raisins
- 1 cup currants
- ½ cup mixed candied fruit, chopped
- 1 cup slivered almonds
- ¼ cup finely chopped almonds
- 2 tablespoons light corn syrup
- 2 tablespoons water

Sift flour with baking powder, salt, and spices. Cream margarine, add sugar gradually, cream until light and fluffy. Add eggs, one at a time, beating well after each addition. Then add flour mixture alternately with orange juice, beginning and ending with dry ingredients. Beat after each addition until smooth. Fold in fruit and slivered almonds.

Spread batter in well-greased 9-inch tube pan or 3-inch-deep 9-inch torte pan. Bake in moderate oven (350°) for 30 minutes, then sprinkle chopped almonds over top of cake. Continue baking 30–35 minutes longer, or until cake is done.

Simmer syrup and water together for one minute, then brush over top of cake to hold almonds in place and to give a gloss. Cool cake 15 minutes in pan, then turn out on rack to finish cooling. Wrap in foil and freeze until time of use or store in refrigerator for at least 24 hours before serving.

Makes 1 cake.

France

Probably the first Christmas celebration in France was in Rheims in A.D. 496 when Clovis and three thousand of his warriors were baptized. More than three hundred years later, on Christmas Day in the year 800, Charlemagne was "Crowned by God the Great and Pacific Emperor," under the auspices of Pope Leo III. Later Baudouin was crowned in the basilica of Saint Marie of Bethlehem; King Jean-le-Bon founded the Order of the Star in honor of the Virgin Mary; crowds welcomed Queen Isabeau of Bavaria with cries of *"Noël! Noël!"*

Gradually historical events gave way to religious and secular observances. Today Christmas is essentially a family day, a religious celebration, a time of gaiety and merrymaking.

Just before midnight on Christmas Eve the French family and their guests of Catholic faith in the Besançon area bundle up in their warmest mufflers and outer coats and walk through the snow, which sparkles in the light of the candle that each one carries to light his way to midnight Mass. Here as in other parts of France, the church is magnificently lighted for the midnight Mass. The crèche is often elaborate and may be of great age. In some

regions of France in earlier times, a baby was placed on the hay of the crèche during the Mass, but this custom, a great favorite with the peasants, is no longer generally observed. At the conclusion of the ceremony people return home to enjoy *le réveillon* or late supper. Here the favorite dish of stuffed goose may be served—in Paris it would be oysters—along with a bountiful variety of delicacies such as *foie gras,* truffles, pastries, and puddings.

Games and dancing usually follow this sumptuous menu. This may continue until early morning. The rest of the day is a quiet one, for Christmas has never been as important a national holiday as New Year's Day in France.

As for children, before they go to bed on Christmas Eve they put their shoes by the fireside, expecting a gift from *le père Noël* or *le petit Jésus.* Formerly *sabots,* peasants' wooden shoes, were popular at Christmas time, but today the shoes set before the fireplace or around the Christmas tree may be of any kind. But the *sabots* are not forgotten, for the pastry shops make chocolate wooden shoes and fill them with candies as a reminder of the old custom.

LA GALETTE DES ROIS
Epiphany Cake

The *Galette des Rois*—literally, the Kings' Cake—is traditionally served in many parts of France on Epiphany, the twelfth day after Christmas, to commemorate the visit of the Three Kings to Bethlehem. The custom, traditional particularly in the provinces north of the Loire River, has become popular because it affords an excuse for an unusual and enjoyable party. The *Galette des Rois* is a round cake made from flaky pastry in which a bean, pea, or other favor is baked. In today's commercially baked cakes, the favor is usually a small charm in the shape of a king. The guest whose piece contains the favor is then the king or queen for the evening, and is given a special crown to wear throughout the evening. The lucky one then kisses the man or woman whom he chooses to reign with him for the evening and wear the other crown. When the *Galette des Rois* is purchased from the *pâtisserie*, the baker always provides two paper crowns with each cake, but many families enjoy making their own elaborate crowns for this occasion. When there is more than one cake served at the Epiphany party, of course there has to be more than one favor and more than one king (and queen).

The base of the *Galette des Rois* is the traditional *Pâte Feuilletée*.

PÂTE FEUILLETÉE
Puff Paste

Through the French consulate in San Francisco, Madame Josephine Araldo has generously shared this recipe with me.

    4   cups flour
    1½   cups water
    1   lb. (2 cups) butter or 1 cup butter, 1 cup margarine
    1   teaspoon sugar
    ⅜   teaspoon salt

Put flour in a bowl and add enough of the water to make soft enough to roll. Flour board, roll paste and in the center place the softened butter. Fold up the four corners to completely envelope the butter. Then roll out in one direction then another to make a square, one inch thick. Then fold again in three folds without separating. Roll again the same way—this operation is termed "turn." Fold again and the paste will have had two turns. (Dent with two finger marks to keep track of turns.) Place in refrigerator in a damp towel and let rest at least 15 to 20 minutes.

Then give two more turns as before; dent with four

marks and let stay in the refrigerator until required. When ready to use give two more turns. This paste is better when made the day before and will keep for three to four weeks in the refrigerator and up to six months in the freezer.

FILLING

- ½ cup sugar
- 2 egg yolks
- 3 whole eggs
- ⅓ cup evaporated milk
- ⅓ cup rum or 1 tablespoon vanilla
- ½ cup softened unsalted butter or margarine
- ½ cup almond paste

Beat sugar, egg yolks, and 3 whole eggs until creamy in color. Add evaporated milk and flavoring, beating to blend.

Roll out puff paste 8 inches in diameter and ¹⁄₁₆ inch thick and fit into 8-inch pie plate or flan ring pan. Spread with almond paste, coating thoroughly but leaving clear a ¾-inch border. Insert whole almond or other favor into any part of paste. Cover with another piece of puff paste of the same dimensions. Seal edges and crimp border. Brush with an egg, lightly beaten. Make a rosette or other design on top of puff pastry with the fine point of a knife. Sprinkle lightly with sugar and bake in a hot oven (400°) 10 minutes. Then lower heat to 350° and bake 25 to 30 minutes longer, until center tests done with toothpick. Remove from oven and sprinkle with 2 tablespoons or more of granulated sugar. Place under broiler for 2 minutes to glaze, watching carefully that sugar does not burn. Or you may sprinkle the *Galette* with confectioners' sugar. Cool before serving.

Note: Various provinces have their special recipe for Galette des Rois. This one is typical of Orleans Province, south of Paris.

Makes two 8-inch cakes.

England also has a Twelfth Night Cake which dates back to olden times. Robert Herrick wrote of it in *Twelfe Night* as follows:

"Now, now the mirth comes
With the Cake full of plums
Where Bean's the king of the sport here,
Besides we must know,
The pea also
Must revell, as Queen, in the Court here."

The recipe which follows is for a kind of English poundcake bursting with fruit.

Twelfth Night Cake

1 cup butter or margarine
¾ cup dark brown sugar, firmly packed
3 eggs
¼ cup thin milk
3 cups flour
¾ cup seeded raisins
¾ cup currants
¾ cup mixed candied fruits
½ teaspoon salt
¼ teaspoon allspice
1 teaspoon cinnamon
¼ teaspoon nutmeg, ground
¼ cup blanched almonds, chopped fine
1 favor

Cream butter and gradually add sugar, beating until light and fluffy. Add eggs one at a time, beating after each addition. Add milk and carefully stir to blend. Sift a little flour over fruit. Sift together dry ingredients and fold into batter as lightly as possible. Fold in fruits and almonds, beating vigorously to blend. Line a round oiled 9-inch tube pan with heavy waxed paper and lightly butter this. Pour batter into pan, insert favor, and bake in a slow oven (250°) for about 2½ hours.

Makes 1 large cake.

ABOUT PAN SIZES AND BAKING TIMES
FOR FRUITED CAKES

Fruitcakes may be baked in all sizes and shapes. To estimate baking time, keep this list of pan sizes and amounts handy.

An $8\frac{1}{2} \times 4\frac{1}{2} \times 2\frac{3}{4}$-inch loaf pan holds about 4 cups and takes about an hour and 50 minutes to bake.

A $5\frac{1}{2} \times 3 \times 2\frac{1}{2}$-inch loaf pan holds about $1\frac{3}{4}$ cups batter and takes about $1\frac{1}{2}$ hours to bake.

A $4\frac{1}{2} \times 1\frac{1}{2}$-inch round pan holds from 1 to $1\frac{1}{4}$ cups of batter and takes about an hour and 25 minutes to bake.

A 3-quart tube pan or mold holds about $2\frac{1}{2}$ quarts of batter and takes from $2\frac{1}{2}$ to 3 hours to bake, depending on tube size.

A $7\frac{1}{2}$-inch ring mold holds 3 cups of batter and takes about an hour and 40 minutes to bake.

A 6-ounce juice can will hold $\frac{1}{2}$ cup batter and bake in about 50 minutes.

Cupcake pans measuring $1\frac{3}{4} \times \frac{3}{4}$ inches will each hold a heaping tablespoon of batter and will take about 20 minutes to bake.

Slow baking is the key for successful fruitcakes. In general the oven should be set between 250° and 325°, depending on the type of cake and size of pan used.

Put a pan of warm water on bottom rack of oven for first 45 minutes of baking time to prevent cracking.

WHITE FRUITCAKE—SOUTHERN STYLE

- 1   cup sugar
- 1   cup butter or margarine
- 4   egg yolks
- 2½ cups sifted flour
- 1   teaspoon baking powder

1 teaspoon nutmeg
½ teaspoon salt
1 teaspoon sherry
½ teaspoon almond extract
1 cup chopped nutmeats
½ cup citron, orange, or lemon peel, finely sliced
½ cup finely shredded coconut, if desired
1 cup white raisins
¼ cup chopped candied pineapple
¼ cup pitted dates, cut into small pieces
¼ cup maraschino cherries
4 egg whites

Sift sugar and beat in butter, blending them carefully together until creamy and light in color. Add egg yolks, beating them in one at a time. Resift flour with other dry ingredients. Add sherry and almond extract to butter-sugar mixture, and stir to blend. Stir the dry ingredients slowly into the batter, mixing well after each addition. Stir in nutmeats, candied fruits, coconut. When these are thoroughly blended, add at very last the egg whites, beaten until stiff but not dry, folding carefully into batter. Bake the cake in a greased 9-inch tube pan in a slow oven (325°) until it is done (about one hour). Put a pan of warm water on bottom rack of oven for first 45 minutes of baking time to prevent cracking. Add Sugar Glaze (page 158) a week before use, if desired.

Makes one 9 × 3-inch round cake or 3 or 4 small ones.

DARK FRUITCAKE

1½ cups chopped nutmeats
½ pound (1½ cups) blanched almonds
2 pounds (about 4 cups) candied fruit mix
1 pound (2¾ cups) seedless raisins
½ pound (about 1⅓ cups) currants
2 tablespoons or more brandy
½ cup orange marmalade

¼ teaspoon allspice
2 teaspoons cinnamon
¼ teaspoon cloves
1 teaspoon nutmeg
½ pound (1 cup) butter or margarine
½ pound (1⅛ cups) dark brown sugar
½ cup dark molasses
6 eggs, separated
1 cup figs, cut small
1 cup pitted dates, chopped
½ pound (about 1¾ cups) flour
1 teaspoon baking soda
1 teaspoon salt

Chop nuts and add to candied fruit, raisins, and currants. Add brandy, marmalade, and spices. In another bowl cream butter, then add sugar, and beat until thoroughly blended. Add molasses and egg yolks which have been previously beaten until foamy. Blend and pour over fruit mixture. Stir in figs and dates. Resift flour, baking soda, and salt and add to mixture, beating vigorously. Adjust flour and seasonings as desired. *Be sure dough is firm, not runny.*

Grease pans thoroughly, line with waxed paper, and grease this too. Fill pans two-thirds full and bake in a slow oven (275°), as outlined on page 124, until firm.

Turn cakes onto wire rack and remove paper. While warm pour about ¼ cup brandy over each cake—gradually so that it can be absorbed. Glaze as desired and decorate with almonds and candied fruits. Let cool. Wrap and store in an air-tight container. If Sugar Glaze (page 158) is used, glaze cake one week before use.

Makes 5 pounds.

GERMAN APPLE BUNDT CAKE

This old German favorite has gone through many adaptations over the years but continues to be a favorite because of its texture and taste. In reality it is a very enriched coffeecake, but it is equally at home at a coffee, tea, or teen-agers' gathering. It cuts into thin slices which can be easily spread with butter or margarine, and it is sweeter than bread, yet not as sweet as a regular cake, and has a robust spiciness to distinguish it from the commonplace.

2 cups applesauce, seasoned with ¼ teaspoon ground caraway
1 package (9 ounces) dried mincemeat
2 envelopes active dry yeast
½ cup lukewarm water
1 cup warm milk
2 tablespoons sugar
3 tablespoons vegetable oil
2 teaspoons salt
1 cup walnut meats, chopped fine
7½ cups sifted flour
Confectioners' Sugar Icing (p. 156)

Mix applesauce with crumbled mincemeat and cook until mixture is thick. Cool. Add yeast to lukewarm water and let stand without stirring for 5 minutes. Stir yeast to blend well. Mix milk, sugar, oil, and salt. Stir to blend, and cool to lukewarm. Stir in dissolved yeast and nuts. Stir in apple-mincemeat mixture. Gradually beat in flour until a stiff dough is formed that is just manageable. Turn out on a lightly floured board and knead until dough is satiny and elastic. Put dough in an oiled bowl, cover with cloth and let rise in a warm place until double in bulk (about 1½ hours). Punch dough down and shape into a long roll, long enough to fit into a well-oiled Bundt pan or a 10-inch by 4-inch tube pan. Let rise until almost double in bulk. Bake in a moderate oven (350°) for 40 to 45 minutes or until cake sounds hollow when tapped. Cool on a rack. Spoon Confectioners' Sugar Icing over top.
Makes 1 cake.

Old-fashioned gingerbread has been a traditional Christmas delicacy for a long time, and the gingerbread house or castle was a feature of earlier times.

In my childhood home two types of gingerbread were made. The soft variety was quite cakelike and was served in 3-inch squares. As a special treat, occasionally it was broken into small pieces in a glass or bowl of milk and the combination was spooned. Absolutely delicious!

Then there was a second variety that was made into ginger cookies or snaps and shaped variously to hang on the Christmas tree or to serve with other cookies to holiday guests.

In *The White House Cook Book* of 1905 Hugo Ziemann and Mrs. F. L. Gillette gave the following "receipt" for a soft Ginger Cake:

"Stir to a cream one cupful butter and half a cupful of brown sugar; add to this two cupfuls of cooking molasses, a cupful of sweet milk, a tablespoonful of ginger, a teaspoonful of ground cinnamon; beat all thoroughly together. Then add three eggs, the whites and yolks beaten separately; beat into this two cups of sifted flour, then a teaspoonful of soda dissolved in a spoonful of water and last two more cupfuls of sifted flour. Butter and paper two square breadpans, divide the mixture and pour half into each. Bake in a moderate oven. This cake requires long and slow baking from 40 to 60 minutes. I find that if sour milk is used the cakes are much lighter, but either sweet or sour milk is excellent."

SOUR CREAM GINGERBREAD

2   cups sifted flour
1   teaspoon soda
1   teaspoon double-acting baking powder
½   teaspoon salt
1½ teaspoons ginger
¾   teaspoon cinnamon
¼   teaspoon allspice
½   cup brown sugar, firmly packed
2   eggs
½   cup dark molasses
1   cup sour milk or buttermilk
½   cup softened shortening

Sift flour, soda, baking powder, salt, spices, and sugar into a bowl. Mix well. Beat eggs until foamy and stir in molasses, sour milk, and shortening. Stir gradually into the flour-sugar mixture, beating until smooth. Batter should be thin. Turn into a greased 8 × 11-inch baking pan. Bake in a preheated moderate oven (350°) for 40 to 50 minutes. Cut in squares and serve warm, plain or topped with applesauce or whipped cream.

For a crisper, candied crust, bake at 375° for 20 minutes, then reduce to 300° and bake 20 minutes more.

Makes one 8 × 11-inch cake.

PAIN D'ÉPICE
Gingerbread

M. F. K. Fisher, the distinguished American author of *Serve It Forth* and other books about food and gastronomy, and believer that food can be, and quite often is, a mysterious, important part of turning us into something more than the "beasts of the field," has this to say about gingerbread as made in Dijon, France. "All year and everywhere we smelled the Dijon gingerbread, that *pain d'épice* which came perhaps from Asia with a tired Crusader.

"Its flat strange odour, honey, cow dung [used as a fuel in many parts of Europe], clove, something unnamable but unmistakable, blew over all the town. Into the theatre sometimes would swim a little cloud of it, or quickly through a café grey with smoke. In churches it went for one triumphant minute far above the incense."

Mrs. Fisher gives the recipe which follows and which is used with the permission of The World Publishing Company.

"Take two pounds of old black honey [the Europeans used to let their honey stand for a year before using it], the older and blacker the better, and heat it gently. When it has become a thin liquid, stir it very slowly and thoroughly into two pounds of the finest bread flour, of which about one-third is rye.

"Put this hot paste away in a cold place. It must stay there for at least eight days, but in Dijon, where *pain d'épice* is best, it ripens in the cold for several months or even years!

"Wait as long as you can, anyway. Then put it in a bowl and add six egg yolks, one level teaspoon of carbonate of soda, and three teaspoons of bicarbonate of soda.

"Next comes the seasoning—and it is there, I think, that lies the magic. Try these the first time, before you begin your own experimenting: some pinches of anise, a teaspoon dry mustard, and the zest of a large lemon.

"Now beat it for a painfully long time. Put it in a buttered mould or pan and bake it in a moderate oven for one hour—or less if you have divided this measure into more than one pan."

Mrs. Fisher goes on to recount that in Dijon the sliced gingerbread is spread with marmalade and glazed, or large loaves are thin-sliced and coated with apricot jam and then put together again. Sometimes currants and candied fruits are added to the basic dough and baked into the loaves. Or the big loaves are left plain and cut into thin slices and buttered with sweet butter to serve with coffee or tea.

Mrs. Fisher cautions against premature use of this fragrant delicacy, stating that it should be wrapped in waxed paper and stored in a tightly covered box for a couple of months or more for a mellowing of flavors.

MUSTARD GINGERBREAD

As Mrs. Fisher suggests, you can go creative with your own seasonings for this old-time favorite. If you want to experiment with the addition of mustard (and I can recommend it), remember that this seasoning sometimes enhances other flavors at the expense of its own aroma.

To speed you on your way, listed below is an old recipe that does include mustard in its ingredients.

2   cups flour
¼   cup rye flour
2   teaspoons baking powder
½   teaspoon salt
½   cup shortening or margarine
½   teaspoon soda
1   teaspoon anise seed
1   teaspoon cinnamon
1   teaspoon ginger
½   teaspoon dry or 1 rounded teaspoon prepared Dijon
      mustard
½   cup brown sugar
1   cup unsulfured molasses
1   large egg
1   cup hot water

Sift together flours, baking powder, and salt. Cut shortening into small pieces. Add soda and spices to shortening and carefully blend 2 minutes at low speed. Gradually beat in sugar and molasses. Beat in egg. Add flour mixture alternately with hot water, beating after each addition. Pour batter into a greased and floured 9-inch-square pan. Bake in a preheated moderate oven (350°) about 45 minutes until a toothpick inserted in center comes out clean. Cool in pan 10 minutes. Turn onto wire rack to complete cooling, or serve warm with fruit, whipped cream or other topping such as Cranberry Whipped Cream.

Makes one 9-inch square, 9 servings.

CRANBERRY WHIPPED CREAM

Courtesy of Cranberry Kitchen of the National Cranberry Association, and simply delectable.

    1   cup heavy cream
    1   tablespoon lemon juice
    1   cup jellied cranberry sauce, crushed with a fork
    ¼   cup confectioners' sugar, sifted

Whip heavy cream until stiff. Fold in lemon juice. Lightly fold in crushed cranberry sauce and confectioners' sugar. Serve as topping for hot gingerbread.

Note: A commercial whipped topping may be substituted for heavy cream if desired.

GRANDMA'S CARROT APRICOT-JAM CAKE

This is a moist cake of excellent keeping quality which has proved to be one of my most popular cakes for festive occasions. It can be varied with the nuts and jam you use, providing the jam is thick. Until this year I have followed Grandma's practice of spreading the cake with apricot jam. However, German-born Petra Wertz tells me that

in Central Europe plum jam is generally used for tartness and flavor accent. Whether Grandma knew this, I'll never know. She did have an apricot tree and a walnut tree in her home garden, and she was a provident woman. Need I say more?

1⅓ cups water
1⅓ cups sugar
1 cup raisins
3 cups grated carrots
1 tablespoon margarine
½ teaspoon cinnamon
½ teaspoon cloves
¼ teaspoon mace
⅛ teaspoon salt
2 cups sifted flour
1 teaspoon soda
1 teaspoon baking powder
½ cup walnut meats, cut small
½ cup or more apricot jam

Put first nine ingredients into a large saucepan and cook over medium heat for 10 minutes. Remove from heat and let cool. Meanwhile sift together flour, soda, and baking powder and add to carrot mixture, mixing thoroughly. Stir in nutmeats. Pour batter into a 9- or 10-inch lightly greased and floured square cake pan. Bake in a slow oven (300°) for 1 hour or more, until it tests done. Let cool and spread with ½ cup apricot jam (be sure cake is cold to avoid sogginess). Over this spread Brown Sugar Frosting (page 156).

Makes one square 9- or 10-inch cake.

HONING KOEK
Dutch Honey Cake

This is an old Dutch recipe that came to me from Mrs. W. J. van Heekeren, by way of her niece Adele Matthias Nederburgh of Pasadena, California. This pleasantly spiced loaf cake should be sliced thin and lightly buttered. It is such a nice addition to all the rich breads of the Christmas season that I particularly appreciate the generosity of these friends in letting me share it with you.

3	tablespoons honey (heaping)
2½	cups light brown sugar
1¼	cups milk
4	cups flour
1	teaspoon salt
1	teaspoon baking powder
1	teaspoon soda
½	teaspoon cinnamon
½	teaspoon nutmeg
½	teaspoon ground cloves

Mix honey, sugar, and milk together. Sift together dry ingredients and stir into honey mixture. Pour into two well-greased 9 × 5 × 3-inch bread pans. Bake in slow oven (300°) for about 1 hour or until done.

Makes 2 loaf cakes.

ORANGE GLAZED DATE CAKE

I am indebted to Mrs. Howard Green of Oakland, California, for the use of this excellent date cake recipe which is similar to the old *Gâteau des Dattes* recipe and, in my opinion, a little more delicate. A moist cake, this is a good do-ahead recipe for busy December homemakers.

　1½　cups (¾ pound) margarine
　1½　cups sugar
　3　eggs
　3¾　cups unsifted flour
　1½　teaspoons baking powder
　1½　teaspoons soda
　¾　teaspoon salt
　1¼　cups buttermilk
　2　tablespoons Curaçao (optional)
　1　cup chopped dates
　1　cup chopped walnuts
　1½　tablespoons grated orange peel
　2　tablespoons flour
　　Orange Glaze (page 158)

Using the large bowl of electric mixer, cream together the margarine and sugar. Beat in the eggs. Mix the flour, baking powder, soda, and salt; add alternately with the buttermilk, mixing at low speed to blend after each addition. Sprinkle Curaçao over dates, nuts, and orange peel; dust with 2 tablespoons flour and stir into batter. Turn into a buttered 9- or 10-inch tube pan and bake in a moderate oven (350°) about 1½ hours or until the cake starts to pull away from the sides of the pan.

Remove from oven, and while still hot pierce the cake all over with an ice pick or skewer. Slowly spoon the hot orange glaze over the cake until it is all absorbed. Cool thoroughly before removing from pan. Serve with whipped cream.

Makes 1 cake—12 servings.

POUNDCAKE

British in origin, the poundcake often featured currants, candied fruits, and lemon extract. However, the old-fashioned poundcake that our grandmothers made was plain and rich with butter and sugar, and was popular in America as well as in England for high tea or fruit accompaniment in December or any month. A very stiff batter, it required long beating. Today the drudgery is taken out of the preparation of this cake by the use of the electric mixer. All you will need are the ingredients and a generous half hour of time. This is one cake for which I do use butter.

As cupcakes were named for having their ingredients measured by the cupful, so the poundcake got its name from the pound measurements that were used to designate amounts of ingredients to be used, according to Amelia Simmons in *American Cookery.*

My 1905 *The White House Cook Book* admonishes the cook to store her poundcake in an earthen jar, tightly covered, "first dipping letter paper in brandy and placing it over the top of cake." It is an excellent cake for flavor, texture, and keeping qualities. The ingredients called for in an old recipe would have read about like this, but the preparation steps would have been quite different:

1 pound butter
1 pound sugar
9 medium eggs (1 pound), separated
4 cups sifted cake flour (1 pound)
¼ teaspoon baking powder
¼ teaspoon salt
1 teaspoon grated nutmeg
1 pound candied fruit (Danish addition—optional)

Cream butter for 15 minutes. Add sugar slowly, beating until fluffy and light lemon in color (about 10 minutes). Beat into butter mixture the egg yolks, beating well to blend. Add flour, baking powder, salt, and nutmeg; mix well. Fold in egg whites (and candied fruit, if used) and blend. Pour batter into two well-greased 9 × 5 × 3-inch loaf pans. Bake in a preheated slow oven (325°) 55 to 60 minutes.

Makes 2 loaf cakes.

MRS. SHIRES'S POUNDCAKE

Mrs. Henry Shires, widow of the late Suffragan Bishop of the Diocese of California of the Episcopal Church, served tea to hundreds of church friends and the clergy as the wife of one of California's beloved church leaders. She enjoyed cooking as much as she did entertaining and was also most generous in sharing her recipes. Her pound-cake which follows, although very different in texture from the usual poundcake, is delicious. I have served it for years with eggnog, tea, coffee, or hot cocoa. Unlike the usual loaf poundcake, Mrs. Shires's cake is baked in a tube pan.

2¾ cups sifted cake flour
1¾ cups sugar
2   teaspoons double-acting baking powder
1½ teaspoons salt
1   cup vegetable shortening (butter may be substituted)
¾   cup milk
4   large eggs
2   teaspoons vanilla
1   teaspoon lemon extract

In a big bowl put the flour, sugar, baking powder, salt, shortening, milk, and 2 eggs. Beat 2 minutes at medium speed. Add 2 more eggs. Beat 2 minutes at higher speed. Add vanilla and lemon extracts. Grease well and flour lightly a 9-inch tube pan, and pour batter into pan. Bake in a moderate oven (375°) for 45 minutes. Invert and cool on rack. Store in covered cake container.

Makes one 9-inch cake—20 or more slices.

Note: I often add ¼ teaspoon mace to dry ingredients.

Yorkshire, the largest of England's counties, has three distinct areas within it. Each one has its own dialect and customs, and each makes a spice cake according to local traditions.

Spice, Yule, and Pepper Cake are some of the names applied to this Christmas loaf which fairly bursts with raisins, currants, candied peels, and spices. Yorkshire housewives cherish the old superstition that they will have as many happy months in the year to come as they have requests for their spice cake.

YORKSHIRE SPICE CAKE

1   cup sugar
½   cup margarine
½   cup lard or vegetable shortening

¼ nutmeg, grated
½ lemon, grated rind and juice
1 cup currants
1 cup raisins
¼ cup mixed candied peels, cut small
3½ cups pastry flour
2 teaspoons baking powder
3 eggs, separated
   About ½ cup milk
1 egg white

Cream together sugar, margarine, lard, and nutmeg until fluffy. Dredge fruits with some of the flour. Sift remaining flour with baking powder. Beat egg yolks until thick and add to creamed mixture. Now add flour, alternating with milk. Fold in fruits and beat vigorously. Last, fold in beaten egg whites. Pour into greased bread tin lined with waxed paper. Glaze with egg white. Bake about 1½ hours in slow oven (300°). Decorate top with blanched almonds and candied fruits or top with a syrup glaze or frosting.

Makes one 9 × 5 × 3-inch long cake or 2 smaller ones.

SUGAR CAKE

Mrs. F. F. Couch of Bethlehem, Pennsylvania, has shared a number of Moravian and German recipes with me, including one for Sugar Cake. Mrs. Couch says it should be considered a coffee or tea cake, and the brown sugar dressing adds richness to it.

1 cup hot, dry mashed potatoes
1 cup sugar
1 cake yeast dissolved in 1 cup lukewarm water
½ cup melted butter or margarine
¼ cup softened butter
½ cup brown sugar
1 teaspoon cinnamon
½ cup lard, melted

2   eggs, lightly beaten
¼   teaspoon salt
4   cups flour

Mix ingredients in order of listing and put into a lightly greased, large bowl. Cover with dampened cloth and let rise in a warm room. This may take as long as 3 hours or more. Spoon batter into 4 greased bread pans. Cover and let rise until light (about 1 or more hours). Bake in a moderate oven (350°) for 30 to 40 minutes, until golden brown. Remove from oven and dot tops of loaves with ice-pick holes, spacing them about 1 inch apart and not too deep. Put a dot of butter into each hole; melt remaining butter and brush top of each loaf. Plug holes with brown sugar as soon as butter has bubbled up and sprinkle tops lightly with brown sugar and cinnamon. Let cool and turn onto racks. Store.

Makes 4 small loaves.

YULE LOG
Bûche de Noël

The French Yule Log, *Bûche de Noël,* is a symbolic cake which is now sold by all French confectioners, according to Prosper Montaigne in *Larousse Gastronomique.* The cake is generally made of a *Génoise* type of pastry, and is spread with butter-cream filling, rolled into a log, frosted and decorated to look like a log of wood reminiscent of the yule log that used to be burned in the fireplace on Christmas Eve.

Light as a feather, this cake is a foreign cousin to our jelly and chocolate rolls. It is traditionally featured in Paris and the Ile-de-France region along with oysters and *foie gras* in the late Christmas Eve supper or *réveillon* which is served on the family's return from midnight Mass.

For superlative results use a heavy metal whisk for "beating" eggs in order to get the greatest amount of

air into them. Eggs must be at room temperature and mixing bowl and whisk (or beaters) should be warm, never cold. Authentically, no baking powder should be used in this cake for its lightness depends upon the careful folding of the perfectly beaten egg whites into the batter. The recipe that follows is a modern version using pancake mix. I have used a regular pancake mix and a Swedish pancake mix in this recipe and believe the latter gives a finer product.

4 eggs
2 tablespoons unsweetened cocoa
½ teaspoon salt

¾   cup sugar
1   teaspoon vanilla
¾   cup pancake mix
     Mocha Butter Cream Frosting (page 157)

Beat eggs until light and lemon-colored. Combine cocoa, salt, and sugar, and add gradually to egg mixture while continuing to beat. Stir in vanilla. Add pancake mix and beat until smooth. Prepare a 15 × 10 × 1-inch jelly roll pan by greasing it thoroughly, including the sides, then lining it with waxed paper and greasing that. Spread batter evenly over this. Bake in a preheated hot oven (400°) for 12 minutes. Test with finger in center of roll. If imprint remains, cake is done. Loosen edges of cake and turn out onto a clean kitchen towel generously sprinkled with sifted confectioners' sugar. Peel off paper and trim edges, if necessary, then carefully roll up cake and towel. Let cool, then carefully unroll towel and cake and lightly spread cake with ⅓ of the Mocha Butter Cream. Keep remaining frosting in refrigerator until time of use. Roll cake again without towel, wrap in foil, and freeze. To serve, frost with the remaining Mocha Butter Cream. Mark sides and top with tip of knife to resemble tree bark. Cut off a thin slice from end of roll. Unroll, cut in half, and reroll to make two little "stumps." Place these on top of "log" near each end. Sprinkle with pistachio nuts and flaked coconut or white sugar crystals to resemble snow.

Makes 1 roll of 10 to 12 slices.

CHERRY TORTE
Black Forest Style

This Cherry Torte, Black Forest style, might just suit you as a special dessert for a bridge party or a luncheon. It is two layers of delicate spongecake put together with a tasty cherry filling and a butter-cream frosting over all.

4 eggs
2 cups sugar
½ teaspoon salt
2 teaspoons vanilla
2 tablespoons melted butter or margarine
1 cup boiling hot milk
2 cups sifted cake flour
2 teaspoons baking powder

Beat eggs until very light. Beat in sugar, salt, and vanilla. Add butter and hot milk, mixing well. Stir together flour and baking powder; quickly beat into egg mixture. Pour into two greased and floured 9-inch layer cake pans. Bake in preheated moderate oven (350°) for about 25 minutes or until done. Let stand in pan 5 minutes, then turn out on rack to cool before adding filling and frosting.

FILLING

1 16-ounce can pitted dark sweet cherries
⅓ cup kirsch or cherry brandy
1½ tablespoons cornstarch

Drain cherries, reserving ¾ cup syrup. Halve cherries and pour kirsch or cherry brandy over them; let stand 2 hours. Place cornstarch in saucepan; gradually blend in syrup. Cook, stirring, until mixture thickens and comes to a boil. Cook and stir 1 minute. Add cherry mixture. Cool. Chill.

BLACK FOREST BUTTER CREAM

½ cup soft butter
½ cup soft margarine
1 16-ounce package confectioners' sugar
3 egg yolks

Beat butter, margarine, and sugar together until smooth. Beat in egg yolks.

Place one layer of cake on serving plate. Using about

1 cup Butter Cream, make a ½-inch border 1¼ inches high around outer rim of cake. Spread chilled cherry filling in center. Place second layer of cake on top. Frost top and sides of cake with remaining Butter Cream frosting. Decorate sides of cake with chocolate shot, top of cake with chocolate curls shaved from 1 square unsweetened chocolate, and candied cherries.

Makes 1 torte, serving 8 to 10.

CHERRY TORTE

I came upon an old Acadian recipe for a different kind of cherry torte in a Louisiana newspaper several years ago, and have made it almost every Christmas since then, thinking of the "Cherry Tree Carol" as I do so. In this old English air Mary asked Joseph "with her sweet lips so mild" to:

"Pluck those cherries, Joseph

For to give to my Child."
When Joseph refused, Mary commanded the cherry tree
to bend down to her knee.
"That I may pluck cherries
By one, two, and three."
From then on the cherry with its Christmas redness
was used in confections, was candied for use in many
puddings and cakes, and was featured with cinnamon
spicing for its luscious goodness and its gay Christmas
color.

⅔ cup (about 6½ ounces) butter
¼ cup sugar
1 egg
1¾ cups (½ pound) flour

Cream butter and sugar and add egg. Beat to blend.
Fold in flour and mix thoroughly. This is a very rich
dough which crumbles easily. Pat into spring-form pan
or 9-inch cake pan with removable bottom. Press down so
that dough is firm.

FILLING

3 egg yolks
¼ cup sugar
1 cup (½ pint) cream
1 No. 2½ can red pie cherries drained and sprinkled with:
½ teaspoon cinnamon

Beat egg yolks until lemon colored, fold in sugar, pour
in cream. Pour mixture over drained, flavored cherries
and stir gently to combine. Pour over top of dough. Bake
15 minutes in preheated moderate oven (375°).

TOPPING

4 egg whites
6 ounces powdered sugar
½ cup chopped almonds

Beat egg whites stiff but not dry. Add powdered sugar

gradually, blending thoroughly. Spread over cherry mixture and sprinkle generously with almonds. Bake at 350° another hour.

Makes one 9-inch torte, serving 8 to 12.

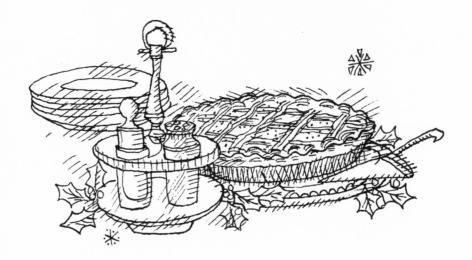

LINZERTORTE

The old recipe listed below was brought to America from Germany in 1830 by Mrs. Bradley Brown's great grandmother. I have been privileged to be served this rich spiced torte for many years and can therefore recommend it as one of the finest Christmas "cakes" you can find. Interestingly, Mr. Brown is the "first assistant" to Mrs. Brown in the making of this torte in their Berkeley, California, kitchen. A man's strong hands are helpful in the final mixing of the thick dough!

4 cups flour
4 teaspoons baking powder
3 teaspoons cinnamon
2 teaspoons nutmeg

1½   teaspoons allspice
1   teaspoon ground cloves
¾   teaspoon mace
¾   teaspoon salt
1½   cups (½ pound) blanched almonds, grated
1¼   cups (½ pound) citron
1   cup (2 sticks) softened butter or margarine
2   cups sugar
3   eggs
2   teaspoons grated lemon rind
¼   cup brandy
1   large glass currant or other tart jelly or jam
1   egg, beaten slightly

In one bowl sift flour, baking powder, spices, and salt. Then stir in the grated nuts and citron. In another bowl cream together the butter and sugar. Beat eggs, add to creamed mixture. Add lemon rind and brandy. Then combine contents of both bowls and knead with hands in bowl until smooth. Dough will be very thick and sticky. Form into a ball, wrap in waxed paper, and store in refrigerator overnight.

Divide dough into four equal parts and work with each separately. On a lightly floured board roll out one part to ¼-inch thickness and fit into a 9-inch buttered flan ring or pie plate. Spread entire surface generously with currant jelly. Make six small balls of dough left after excess has been trimmed. Roll each one between the palms to make strips for lattice. (Do not roll flat into strips as the round, slightly flattened "rope" crisscross is characteristic of this recipe.) Arrange over pie plate, trimming to required length. Use remaining dough to form an edge around baking pan; crimp to hold in place. Brush pastry with slightly beaten egg to glaze. Bake in a moderate oven (375°) about 30 minutes, until golden brown on top. Remove from pie plate when slightly warm.

Repeat process until you have four 9-inch tortes, each

serving 6 to 8 for dessert, 10 to 12 with a beverage like tea or chocolate. For a dessert, serve warm with cheese or vanilla ice cream.

Note: This may be made well ahead of use, wrapped in foil, and frozen until time of use when it should be reheated.

MOHNTORTE
Poppy Seed Cake

Viennese cakes date from the Biedermeier period (1815–1848) and are concocted first to please the eye with spun-sugar decorations and glazed icings. They also please the palate. Originally reserved for the court and bakery shops, they were soon adopted by Viennese housewives. Families pride themselves on their special recipes for Christmas entertaining. One of the favorites is *Mohntorte*.

⅔ cup sugar
6 large eggs, separated
1 cup poppy seeds, finely ground
¼ cup candied citron, chopped very fine
1 teaspoon vanilla

Beat sugar with egg yolks, adding one at a time and beating after each addition. Fold in poppy seeds, candied citron, and vanilla. At the very last fold in stiffly beaten egg whites, handling gently to blend. Pour into a buttered and floured 8-inch cake pan and bake in preheated slow oven (300°) 45 minutes. Remove and cool. Top with Sacher Chocolate Frosting (page 152) or with raspberry jam.

Makes one 8-inch torte.

RASPBERRY TORTE

Scandinavian-inspired, this torte is another of those excellent do-aheads. The jam gives it a Christmas color

and richness, yet the torte is not too rich in company with other baked specialties for a coffee klatch or high tea gathering for December, April, June, or November.

1⅓ cups flour
1 teaspoon baking powder
⅓ cup sugar
½ cup softened margarine
1 large egg
¼ cup (or more) raspberry jam

Blend together dry ingredients; mix in margarine and egg, beating until flour is moistened. Press dough firmly into a round 9-inch flan ring pan with spring-form sides, being sure to cover bottom and sides. Spread jam over dough to cover. Cover and chill while preparing filling.

FILLING

½ cup margarine
⅔ cup sugar
1 cup finely ground almonds and pecan meats
½ teaspoon almond extract
2 large eggs
¼ cup raspberry jam

Cream margarine and sugar, stir in almonds and extract. Add eggs, one at a time, beating well after each addition. Spoon filling over jam-topped dough. Bake about 40 minutes in moderate oven (375°). Cool torte in pan, invert over plate, loosen bottom, and carefully remove from pan. Spread jam over top. Dribble frosting over this; do not spread.

Makes one 9-inch torte, serving 8 to 10.

FROSTING

Mix ½ cup sifted confectioners' sugar and 2 tablespoons lemon juice until smooth.

OLD ENGLISH MINCEMEAT TORTE

1¼ cups sifted flour
½ teaspoon soda
¼ teaspoon salt
1 cup dark brown sugar, firmly packed
2 cups quick-rolled oats
¾ cup softened margarine
2 cups moist mincemeat
3 tablespoons flour
    Grated rind of 1 orange

Sift together the 1¼ cups sifted flour, baking soda, and salt into a mixing bowl. Stir in the brown sugar and oats. Add the margarine. Mix thoroughly. Mix the mincemeat, 3 tablespoons flour, and orange rind. Pat firmly about half (2 cups) of the oatmeal mixture into the bottom of a baking pan 9 × 9 × 1¾. Spread with mincemeat mixture. Pat remaining half of oatmeal mixture over filling. Bake in a moderate oven (350°) 40 minutes, until lightly browned. Cut into 3-inch squares and remove with wide spatula or pancake turner. Serve hot with vanilla ice cream. Or cool in pan placed on wire rack; cut into cooky-size bars, remove with small spatula, and serve with flavored whipped cream or topping.

Makes nine 3-inch squares.

SACHERTORTE

The Sacher Hotel in Vienna has often been called the "Hotel Hapsburg" because in former times the Hapsburg nobility gathered there in good times and bad to dine in imperial fashion. Franz Sacher is thought to have been the originator of the famous cake which bears the family name. Herr Sacher is credited with saying that Prince Metternich bothered him to invent something new. "So what could I do—I just fling together some ingredients—and there you are."

Many credit the *Sachertorte* to his famous wife Anna, who has been memorialized in the play *Reunion in Vienna.* In real life she was anything but the conventional hotel proprietress. She was a fierce little old lady who spent much of her time in later years in a wicker chair outside the hotel entrance, puffing a big cigar, holding securely under one arm a snarling little bulldog while extending a hand to be kissed by reverent young aristocrats entering the hotel. She adored her patrons and fed the impoverished nobility when they could not afford to pay, often letting the *nouveau riche* wait to be served. She had no use for them, only for the nobility. Certainly Anna Sacher was to the Danube monarchy a synonym for luxurious living and eating.

Everyone likes the famous torte that bears the Sacher name. And almost everyone with German or Austrian ancestors claims to have an original recipe for it. Actually the original recipe was published in full, with the permission of Mr. Edward Sacher, Jr., in *Die Wiener Konditorei* by Hans Skrach, quoting among its ingredients eighteen egg whites and fourteen egg yolks.

Housewives have their own versions, and one that I think is excellent is from Frau Willman of Vienna. With a few adaptations, here is the recipe for the famous cake.

SACHERTORTE

5   ounces sweet chocolate
1   tablespoon water
¾   cup (1½ sticks) unsalted margarine or butter
6   eggs, separated
1   cup confectioners' sugar
1¼   cups sifted cake flour
½   teaspoon cinnamon
⅓   cup warm apricot jam

Break the chocolate into small pieces and place in the top of a double boiler with the tablespoon of water. Cook over hot water until the chocolate melts. Add the margarine and stir to blend. Add the beaten egg yolks, one at a time, beating constantly. Add ½ cup sugar and beat steadily until well mixed. Cool for 10 minutes. Beat the egg whites until stiff but not dry. Fold in remaining ½ cup sugar. Fold in the chocolate mixture and the flour-cinnamon alternately, gently but thoroughly. Pour the mixture into an 8-inch or 9-inch spring-form pan that has been buttered and dusted with flour. Bake in a preheated slow oven (325°) for 30 minutes, or until a cake tester comes out clean. Remove from the pan and allow to cool for 30 minutes. Remove spring edge of pan and invert cake on rack. Finish cooling. Slice cake into three layers and spread two layers with Sacher Chocolate Frosting. Put layers together with smooth bottom of cake on top. Spread top and sides with apricot jam and let set 15 minutes. Pour remaining Sacher Chocolate Frosting over the jam. Let stand a day before serving. If you wish to be authentic, add a dollop of whipped cream to each serving.

Makes one 8- or 9-inch torte, serving 8 to 10.

SACHER CHOCOLATE FROSTING

3   ounces unsweetened chocolate or cocoa
1   cup confectioners' sugar

⅓   cup water
½   teaspoon butter or margarine

Combine all ingredients in a large heavy saucepan and cook, stirring, until chocolate is melted. Then cook without stirring to "small thread" stage (230°). Remove from heat, and add butter. Stir constantly until mixture thickens sufficiently to pour over cake, smoothing it on the sides with a knife.

Frostings and Fillings

TO FROST and fill a cake, you will need approximately the following:

For an 8-inch cake—1½ cups
For a 9-inch cake—2 cups
For a 10-inch cake—2¼ to 2½ cups

BUTTER CREAM FROSTING

1   pound confectioners' sugar
½   cup butter or margarine
⅛   teaspoon salt
1   teaspoon vanilla extract
3   to 4 tablespoons milk

Cream one-third of sugar with butter and salt in large bowl. Blend vanilla, 2 tablespoons milk, and remaining sugar into mixture. Gradually stir remaining milk into frosting mixture until desired consistency is reached for spreading.

Makes frosting and filling for one 9-inch cake, the top and sides of a 10-inch tube cake, or the top and sides of a 13 × 9-inch oblong cake.

Note: This basic recipe may be varied in many ways by altering flavoring or adding cocoa, candied cherries, chopped nuts, or angelica.

BROWN SUGAR FROSTING

½   cup brown sugar, firmly packed
2   tablespoons milk
2   tablespoons butter or margarine
⅛   teaspoon salt
¾   cup confectioners' sugar
1   teaspoon vanilla

Combine in a saucepan brown sugar, milk, butter, and salt. Melt and simmer over a low heat for 3 minutes, stirring constantly. Cool and add confectioners' sugar and vanilla. Decorate with walnut or pecan halves, if desired.

MARZIPAN FROSTING

The English poundcake is often frosted with Marzipan Frosting.

1   cup blanched and unblanched almonds
1   pound sifted confectioners' sugar
3   egg whites
1   teaspoon almond extract or 2 teaspoons rose water

Blend almonds in an electric blender. Mix in sugar and thoroughly blend. Beat egg whites until fluffy, then stir into almond mixture. Add almond extract or rose water and mix with hands. If frosting is too stiff for spreading, it may be loosened a little by the addition of more almond extract or fresh lemon juice.

CONFECTIONERS' SUGAR ICING

1   cup sifted confectioners' sugar
1   to 2 tablespoons warm water, milk, or cream
½   teaspoon vanilla or lemon juice (add a bit of grated lemon rind with lemon)

Mix ingredients together to make a smooth icing. Drip over sweet-dough bread while still warm after baking, when extra richness is desired. Decorative candies may be sprinkled over icing for added color.

MOCHA BUTTER CREAM FROSTING

Cream 1½ cups (¾ pound) unsalted margarine. Combine ¾ cup sugar with 1½ tablespoons dark cocoa and 1½ tablespoons instant coffee. Sift through a fine sieve.

Add, a tablespoon at a time, to margarine, continuing to cream until well blended.

Makes sufficient frosting for 1 Yule Log or 1 small cake.

A sugar glaze is a real holiday helper to add flavor to your baked delicacies and also to provide a base for decorating them. Add 2 drops of green vegetable coloring for coating Christmas tree cookies. Then dot with red cinnamon candies, silver balls, fancy mixed sprinkles, or colored sugar crystals. For animal cookies, ice all over the tops or leave plain and simply outline collars or reins or whatever is appropriate with decorative frosting of color desired and stud the trappings with red, green, or silver candies.

ORANGE GLAZE

For fruit bars or fruitcakes

Combine ½ cup sugar and ¼ cup orange juice in small saucepan. Heat and stir until sugar dissolves. Brush to glaze while warm.

LEMON GLAZE

⅓ cup sifted confectioners' sugar
1 tablespoon water
1 teaspoon lemon juice

Blend ingredients together until smooth. Spread on cake or cookies while they are still slightly warm.

SUGAR GLAZE

2 cups sugar
1 cup water
1 tablespoon light corn syrup
Confectioners' sugar

Boil the sugar, water, and corn syrup for 5 minutes. Cool 3 minutes before adding enough confectioners' sugar to make it of spreading consistency. If the glaze gets too hard, add a little hot water. After glazing lightly, decorate with colored candy toppings.

WHITE ICING

Try to make fruitcakes far enough ahead so that they can ripen with flavor before use. This means having them ready for storage not much later than December first. After pricking the baked fruitcakes with an ice pick, skewer, or small knitting needle and sprinkling them with a little brandy or sherry, wrap them in cheesecloth and then in foil. About the middle of the month, repeat the liquor addition to deepen the mellowing process. Add frosting just before use, then decorate with candied red and green cherries, pineapple, citron, angelica, and nuts, as desired.

2 cups sugar
1 tablespoon light corn syrup
⅛ teaspoon salt
½ cup water
2 egg whites
1 teaspoon brandy

Combine sugar, syrup, salt, and water over low heat until sugar is dissolved. Continue boiling until syrup reaches soft ball stage (about 238°). If you do not use a thermometer, drop a small amount of syrup into cold water. If it forms a soft ball between the thumb and fore-finger, it is ready. Beat the egg whites until almost stiff. Add the syrup slowly but in a steady thin stream to the beaten egg whites, beating continuously. Beat until the frosting is of proper consistency to spread. Add brandy for a flavor plus.

WINTER WHITE FROSTING

½ cup sugar
2   tablespoons water
¼ cup light corn syrup
2   large egg whites
1½ teaspoons vanilla
1   teaspoon soft butter

Mix sugar, water, and corn syrup in a saucepan. Cook over low heat. Boil without stirring until syrup spins a thread (234°), keeping pan covered for first three minutes of cooking to prevent crystal formation on sides. While syrup is cooking, beat egg whites until stiff. Pour hot syrup slowly in a thin stream into the beaten egg whites, beating constantly. Add vanilla, 1 teaspoon soft butter, and a few drops of lemon juice if frosting appears at all sugary.

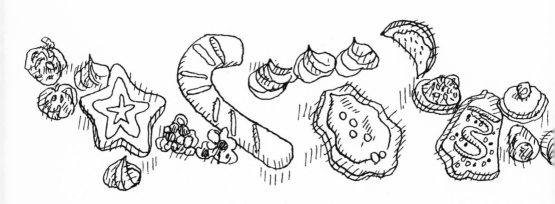

Christmas Means Cookies

COOKIES have played an important part in our holiday food customs for thousands of years. We have
already told how pre-Christian Romans honored Saturn,
their god of sowing, at a mammoth December festival
known as Saturnalia. All business came to a standstill at

this time. Schools were closed. Executions and military activities were temporarily halted. Even slaves were declared "free" for the festival period, which sometimes lasted as long as seven days.

A king of the carnival was chosen by lot, and he presided over the feast. Slaves were allowed to say what they pleased, as a part of their freedom, and their masters ate with them and sometimes even served them. Small gifts were exchanged, the traditional ones being wax candles and clay dolls. One very popular feature was the distribution of little sweet cakes, which may have been the ancestors of our Christmas cookies.

Today Christmas cooky making is a happy tradition for families throughout the western world and each family has its favorites.

The honey pastry *Honigackwerk,* made of flour, honey, ginger and other spices, is a favorite Christmas cooky all over Germany. The stiff dough that is baked very hard is the South German, Swiss, and Scandinavian "picture" cooky called *Springerle.*

The Scandinavians bake their Christmas pastry in the form of a boar or he-goat, *Juleber Julgat.* This is served at Christmas with the other dishes but not eaten until January 19, the feast day of Saint Canute, martyr King of Denmark, who died in 1086.

A familiar Spanish Christmas cooky is the *Dulces de Almendra,* a pastry made of sugar, flour, egg white, and almonds. Similar almond pastries are used during this season in Portugal and Italy.

Central and South American people specialize in the *Buñuelos,* made of white flour and baked or more usually fried to produce a very crisp and brittle cooky. This is often served with syrup or honey.

The French and French Canadians have doughnuts, *Beignets,* made of a special dough, white cream fudge,

Sucre à la Crème, and cakes of whole wheat, brown sugar, and dates, *Carreaux aux Dattes.* The Lithuanian people eat little balls of hard and dried pastry, *Kukuliai,* which are softened in plain water.

Long ago thin wafers signifying the Sacred Host decorated German Christmas trees. Gradually fancy, many-shaped cookies took their place. Among the finest of these were the crisp, white *Christbaumgebäch,* the Christmas tree cooky (page 168). Cookies made from this stiff dough were cut out in the shape of angels, stars, flowers, animals, and figures, and were hung on the Christmas tree along with apples and illuminated with little candles in metal holders. The cookies and fruit were eaten by the children when the tree was taken down in January.

Today many of these specialties of other lands can be bought in bakery shops. But it is so much more fun to bake some cookies at home, particularly if there are young hands to help in the stirring, shaping, and cutting, that I could not give up this pleasant December activity. I repeat certain recipes year after year, and could not bear to leave out any of the family's favorites—a crisp sugar cooky, gingerbread figures, fruit-filled bars, assorted tarts and balls.

Many of these recipes were handed down from my grandmother to my mother to me, and I would like to share some of them with you. Of course I have had to modernize Grandma's instructions, which ran to phrases like "butter the size of a walnut," "a wine glassful," and "a pinch of."

Choose from "Christmas Means Cookies" some recipes for your specialties. Stick to a few cooky recipes in the beginning. Choose one dough for cut-outs, another for drop cookies, and a third for filled or fancy ones. Then go creative with decoration. Before you know it, you will have developed a reputation as a marvelous cook.

ALMOND-CINNAMON ROLLS

2 8-ounce cans almond paste
½ cup confectioners' sugar
1 egg white
1 teaspoon cinnamon

FROSTING

1 egg white
½ cup confectioners' sugar
½ teaspoon vanilla

Mix almond paste and sugar together, using the fingers. Beat egg white until stiff and add cinnamon, then combine with almond paste mixture. Dredge a board or pastry cloth with confectioners' sugar. Roll or pat to ⅛ inch thick. Cut into 3-inch squares. Beat egg white stiff for frosting; add sugar and vanilla. Spread each square with frosting and roll like jelly roll. Place on greased cooky sheet. Bake in preheated slow oven (300°) for 15 to 20 minutes or until lightly browned.
Makes 24 cookies.

Anise is one of the old-time favorite sweet spices of Europe, especially in Germany and the Scandinavian countries. Our modern wedding cake is thought to date back to the anise-flavored cakes served by the Romans after a festive meal.

For our purposes in baking, both the seed and the extract are important additives. But do not overdo. Anise has a powerful flavor, and a little of it goes a long way in baked goods. It is particularly aromatic in such baked items as butter cookies, spritz or springerle-type cookies, sponge or spice cake. To crush the seeds, use a mortar and pestle or place seeds in a measuring cup and crush with back of spoon.

GERMAN ANISE DROPS

2 eggs
1½ cups light brown sugar, firmly packed
2 teaspoons anise seed
¼ teaspoon salt
½ teaspoon soda dissolved in 1 tablespoon hot water
2⅛ cups flour

Beat eggs until very light, add sugar and continue beating. Add anise seed and salt, then dissolved soda and flour. Form dough into small balls the size of hickory nuts, roll in granulated sugar, and place on buttered cooky sheet about 1 inch apart. Bake about 12 minutes at 375°. These cookies improve with age.

Makes about 4 dozen cookies.

APPLE-DATE-RAISIN BARS

This is a rich, fruit-filled cooky that can be made days ahead of use with the assurance that it will be moist and hearty at time of use.

½ cup raisins
1 cup dates
½ cup applesauce
¼ cup sugar
1 cup water
½ teaspoon cinnamon

Mix together and cook over low heat. Stir constantly, to avoid scorching, until mixture is about as thick as mayonnaise, about 5 minutes. Set aside to cool.

BASE AND TOPPING

3 tablespoons vegetable oil
¼ cup light brown sugar, firmly packed
¾ cup sugar
1½ cups sifted flour
1½ cups rolled oats

Put oil and sugars into mixing bowl and blend. Stir in flour and oats. Mix thoroughly. Place half of mixture on lightly greased and floured 8- or 9-inch-square pan. Pat to cover evenly. Spread with cooled filling. Cover with remaining mixture. Pat firmly. Bake in hot oven (400°) about 10 minutes, until golden on top.

Makes 20 cookies.

APRICOT NUT BALLS

An excellent fruit confection from Ethel Vergin's recipe file.

3 cups sugar
½ teaspoon salt
2 cups sour cream
2 cups dried apricots, ground
2 teaspoons vanilla
1 cup chopped walnuts
1 cup finely ground walnuts

In heavy pan combine sugar, salt, sour cream, and apricots. Cook over medium heat; stir until sugar is dissolved. Continue to cook, stirring frequently, to 236° Fahrenheit on candy thermometer, or until a little in cold water forms a soft ball. Let cool for 10 minutes. add vanilla and chopped nuts. Cool 30 minutes. Beat vigorously with a wooden spoon for 1 minute. Refrigerate 20 minutes. Form mixture into walnut-sized balls. Roll in finely ground nutmeats. Store in a covered container.

Makes 36 balls.

BRANDY SNAPS

These different and delicious cookies are from a recipe given me by Ruby Choy.

- ⅓ cup butter or margarine
- ⅓ cup light brown sugar, firmly packed
- 2 ounces dark corn syrup
- ½ teaspoon ground ginger
- ½ cup flour
- ½ teaspoon lemon juice or brandy

Melt butter with sugar, syrup, and ginger in a saucepan. Remove from heat and sift in flour. Add lemon juice and stir. Spoon onto well-oiled cooky sheet, leaving space for rounds to form. Bake in a preheated hot oven (400°) 8 to 15 minutes. Lift snaps from baking sheet with spatula and roll over a large pencil, or hand roll. Add filling of choice or decorate, if desired.

Makes 12 cookies.

The Marion L. Nielsens, friends who spent a winter in Innsbruck, Austria, reminisce about customs in Tyrolean villages during the Christmas season. Beautiful hand-carved, generations-old Nativity scenes grace every home, and a welcoming wreath is hung on each cottage door to signify that the house is open to anyone who may wish to see the crèche within. Visiting many such homes, the Nielsens saw plate after plate of plain round butter cookies displayed. These were not baked by the resident, as you might expect, but by neighbors. They were told that it is the custom in some parts of the Tyrol to take a plate of cookies to your neighbors as a way of saying, "If I have offended you in any way during the year, I beg your pardon." If the cookies are eaten, it means all is forgiven.

Mrs. F. F. Couch of Bethlehem, Pennsylvania, has given me two excellent old German cooky recipes, one of which is a butter cooky. She tells me that these doughs may be made several days before baking time for proper aging. And they must be stored before use to allow the flavorings to deepen.

CHRISTBAUMGEBÄCH

1   cup butter
2   cups sugar
4   eggs, lightly beaten
3½ to 4 cups sifted flour
¼   teaspoon nutmeg
½   teaspoon cinnamon

Cream butter and sugar together. Add the 4 eggs, one at a time, beating after each addition. Add flour, sifted with nutmeg and cinnamon, to make a stiff dough. Wrap dough in waxed paper and refrigerate at least one day; it is better if it stands longer. Then roll out paper-thin, using a cooky cloth on board and a cloth-covered rolling pin for best results. Cut dough into forms of animals, stars, hearts, little men, etc. Bake on ungreased cooky sheet in a moderate oven (375°) for about 6 minutes. Decorate, if desired, with a sprinkling of sugar frosting or colored sugar. Pierce cooky to make a hole if you are going to use as an ornament on a cooky tree.

Makes about 100 cookies.

BROWN CHRISTMAS COOKIES

1   cup dark corn syrup
1   cup molasses (Brer Rabbit, Green Label)
½   cup butter, melted
1   cup brown sugar, firmly packed
    About 5 cups flour
¼   teaspoon salt
1   tablespoon ground ginger
½   teaspoon ground cloves
1   tablespoon cinnamon
1   scant teaspoon soda in 1 tablespoon vinegar

Heat syrup, molasses, and butter to lukewarm. Stir in sugar. Sift together the flour, salt, and spices, and stir into syrup mixture, blending carefully. Add soda-vinegar and blend. Refrigerate at least two hours to allow batter to get stiff. Turn onto lightly floured board, and roll out dough to paper thinness. Cut into fancy shapes—animals, stars, little men, etc. I use a cloth on my board and on the rolling pin which makes it easier to roll the dough thin. Bake in moderate oven (375°) for 6 minutes.

Makes 75 to 100 cookies depending on size of cutters.

Some other well-known traditional cookies which originated in Germany are *Lebkuchen, Pfeffernüsse, and Zimtsterne*. Many of the old German cooky recipes were made with aged molasses or honey, quite different from our modern products, so that some adaptations have been made, but you will still find these cookies rich and flavorsome.

Lebkuchen, the German honey cakes, were always a great favorite in our home, and I hope you will like this old recipe with a few modern twists.

LEBKUCHEN
Honey Cakes

¾ cup unblanched almonds, finely chopped
⅓ cup candied orange peel, finely chopped
⅓ cup candied lemon peel, finely chopped
   About 3 cups sifted flour
¼ teaspoon soda
1 teaspoon cinnamon
½ teaspoon allspice
½ teaspoon ground cloves
½ teaspoon nutmeg
2 eggs
1 cup sugar
½ cup honey

GLAZE

⅓ cup sifted confectioners' sugar
1 tablespoon water
1 teaspoon lemon juice

Mix first three ingredients together; set aside. Blend next six ingredients together; set aside. Beat eggs and sugar together until the mixture is thick. Work in honey very slowly, beating to blend. Gently fold in the dry ingredients in fourths. Mix in the almond mixture. Let dough refrigerate overnight to age, wrapping it in waxed paper. Turn dough into a greased 15½ × 10½ × 1-inch jelly roll pan and spread evenly to ¼ inch thickness, or make into small balls and flatten out to ¼ inch. Bake on a buttered baking sheet in a preheated moderate oven (350°) 15 to 20 minutes, or until wooden pick comes out clean. Set pan on cooling rack to cool slightly. Meanwhile, blend confectioners' sugar, water, and lemon juice together. When *Lebkuchen* is slightly cooled, spread glaze evenly over top and cut into 3 × 1½-inch bars or glaze balls. Remove bars to cooling racks.

Makes about 36 cookies.

FINSKE BRØD
Finnish Shortbread

1 cup butter
1 cup margarine
1 cup sugar
1 cup sifted flour
¼ teaspoon salt
1 teaspoon vanilla
1 egg
1 cup confectioners' sugar
½ cup chopped blanched almonds

Cream butter and margarine until almost white. Blend in sugar. Stir in flour, salt, and vanilla. Roll out on very lightly floured pastry board in long rolls 1 inch wide. Cut in 2-inch lengths. Score with tines of fork. Make a center indentation on each cooky, brush with egg, sprinkle with confectioners' sugar and chopped almonds. Place on a greased baking sheet and bake in a moderate oven ($375°$) 8 to 10 minutes, until golden brown.

Makes 30 cookies.

KLENÄTER I
Christmas Crullers

The Swedish American Line of fine ships has a large variety of baked specialties to add to your calorie intake if you are traveling on one of their ships in December. Platters and platters of cookies are offered. Here is one of the best of the traditional specialties, given through the kindness of Mr. Carl Hallingren, Manager of Public Relations.

4 egg yolks
¼ cup powdered sugar
3 tablespoons butter

1½   cups flour
1   tablespoon brandy
1   tablespoon lemon rind, grated
     Deep fat for frying

Mix ingredients and stir until well blended. Chill. Turn dough onto floured baking board. Roll out thin. With pastry wheel cut strips ¾ inch wide and 3 inches long. Cut gash in center and twist end through. Fry in deep fat (375°) until light brown. Drain on absorbent paper. This authentic Swedish Christmas delicacy may be served with jam as dessert, or plain with coffee.

Makes 50 crullers.

KLENÄTER II

A traditional recipe from Marta Julin Nielsen's kitchen, these cookies are as pretty to look at as they are good to eat.

¼   cup sugar
5   egg yolks
3   tablespoons melted butter
½   lemon, peel and juice
1   tablespoon whisky or cognac
3   cups flour
1   cup sugar

Stir sugar and egg yolks 2 minutes. Add cooled butter, the finely grated lemon peel, juice, and cognac. Stir in flour and work dough on baking board until it is smooth and holds together. Dough should not be hard. Chill in refrigerator for greater firmness. Roll out dough ⅛ inch thick and to about 3 inches in length in a slanting direction, using a pastry wheel to cut to a diamond point. In each diamond piece, make a slit in center from the two farthest points and pull one end through. Lower crullers, one by one, into deep fat and fry at 350° until golden

brown on both sides. Lift out and drain on paper towel.
Sprinkle with granulated or powdered sugar.

Makes about 60 crullers.

KLETSKOPPEN
Dutch Lacy Almond Cookies

Both Mrs. Nederburgh and Mrs. van Diggelen testify
to the excellence of this Christmas cooky, and I agree.
When dough is of perfect consistency, the cookies spread
out and become very thin in baking. Hence their name.
Crisp and delicious, this is an outstanding cooky.

½ cup (1 stick) butter or margarine
1 cup light brown sugar, firmly packed
1 cup flour
¾ teaspoon cinnamon
1 cup blanched almonds, finely chopped
¼ cup warm water

Cream butter and sugar. Add flour sifted with cinnamon. Stir in almonds and water. Drop by teaspoonfuls

onto an ungreased cooky sheet, allowing 2 inches between cookies. Bake in a preheated slow oven (325°) 10 minutes. Let cool 2 minutes; remove to wire rack to finish cooling.
    Makes 48 or more cookies.

No one knows when the aromatic properties of the clove flowers were first discovered. As early as 255 B.C. the Emperor of China recognized their pervasive sweetness and ordered his courtiers to hold cloves in their mouths when in his presence.

Medieval England and western European countries desperately needed the pungent bouquets since their winter meals consisted primarily of meal and salted meat (in the days before cold storage). Before a winter was over, much of the protein fare spoiled. To cut down on this and to make foods more palatable, the rich were willing, even eager, to pay huge sums for cloves, pepper, cinnamon, and nutmeg (sometimes called the Big Four of the spice business). The sale of these rich-bodied spices brought so much gold that small nations prospered for years simply by controlling the spice trade.

Cloves are a must for Christmas baking and mulled beverages. But they deserve careful treatment. Like all herbs and seasonings, cloves should be used to enhance the flavor of your baked specialty, not obscure it. Ground cloves add a rich pungency to applesauce, prune, and spice cakes; dark fruitcake; honey, oatmeal, and spice cookies; nut or raisin bars, gingersnap and other ginger cookies, molasses cookies; steamed brown bread; spiced muffins. Whole cloves are a zestful addition to many holiday beverages. And they are the traditional topping of the favorite holiday cooky of Greece, *Kourabiedes.*

Dr. Kate Karakitsos, of Athens, Greece, states that the Greek Cloud Cooky is served throughout Greece during the Christmas season. A delicate cooky, you will want to handle it with care.

KOURABIEDES
Greek Cloud Cookies

2   cups unsalted butter
¾   cup confectioners' sugar
1   egg yolk
3   tablespoons brandy
4¼   cups sifted flour (approximately)
60   cloves
      Confectioners' sugar

Cream butter until light and fluffy. Gradually add sugar and beat until well mixed. Add egg yolk and brandy and beat *vigorously*. Work in flour, a little at a time, and beat dough until smooth. (Do not underbeat.) Correct dough, adding up to 4 more tablespoonfuls of flour if necessary, but keep dough soft. Mound into a ball, wrap in waxed paper, and chill in refrigerator at least one-half day. With lightly floured hands and working with just a little of the dough at a time, shape dough into small balls about the size of a walnut (1½ inches). Place on ungreased baking sheet and stick a clove in the top of each. Bake in a preheated moderate oven (350°) 14 minutes. Let cool 10 minutes in pan, then, using broad spatula, remove gently to wire rack to finish cooling. Just before cooling is completed, sift confectioners' sugar lightly over each cooky.
Makes 60 cookies.

KRINGEL

3   hard-boiled egg yolks
1   egg yolk
½   cup sugar
4   tablespoons margarine

4   tablespoons vegetable shortening
2   cups flour
½   teaspoon cinnamon
1   teaspoon citrus peels, chopped fine
1½ teaspoons vanilla
    Egg white

Blend hard-boiled egg yolks and raw egg yolk in blender. Cream together sugar, margarine, and shortening. Add to egg mixture and blend. Remove to mixing bowl and add remaining ingredients. Stir and knead until dough forms a smooth ball. Chill in refrigerator for at least two hours. Turn out onto a canvas-covered board or put between two sheets of waxed paper and roll to ⅛-inch thickness. Cut with a doughnut cutter and place "wreaths" one inch apart on greased cooky sheet. Paint each cooky with egg white and decorate with colored sugar or a sprinkling of finely chopped nutmeats. Bake 8 to 10 minutes in a moderate oven (350°).

Makes about 3 dozen cookies.

LEMON CHRISTMAS TREE COOKIES

From my good friends at Sunkist Growers in Los Angeles comes this crisp, zesty cooky, delicious with any beverage or combined with fancy cookies when an assortment is desired.

2   cups sifted flour
½   teaspoon soda
¼   teaspoon salt
⅓   cup butter or margarine, softened
1   cup sugar
1   egg
1   tablespoon lemon peel, finely grated
3   tablespoons fresh lemon juice
    Confectioners' sugar frosting, tinted
    Colored sugar and candy decorettes

Sift flour, soda, and salt. Mix butter or margarine with sugar, egg, and grated lemon peel until light and fluffy. Mix in flour alternately with lemon juice. Chill dough until firm enough to handle, then work with half of dough at a time, keeping rest in refrigerator. On very lightly floured surface, roll dough ⅛ inch thick. With floured cutters, cut into desired shapes. Bake on greased cooky sheet in moderate oven (375°) 8 to 9 minutes, or until lightly browned. Cool. Frost and decorate with colored sugar and candy decorettes. Using needle and strong thread, carefully string cookies to hang on Christmas tree.

Makes 5 dozen small cookies.

MAKRONEN
German Macaroons

Another recipe from Petra Wertz's cooky file, which I have modified a little for American use.

- 4 egg whites
- ⅞ cup sugar
- 2 tablespoons vanilla
- ⅛ teaspoon cinnamon
- 1 tablespoon ground, blanched almonds
- ⅞ cup shredded coconut

Whisk or beat egg whites until very stiff and able to form peaks. Gradually beat in sugar, vanilla, cinnamon, and ground almonds. Blend. Slowly fold in coconut. Drop by teaspoonfuls onto a greased cooky sheet, leaving 1½ inches between macaroons. Bake in a slow oven (325°) 20 to 25 minutes. Remove to wire racks and cool before storing.

Makes about 36 macaroons.

MERINGUES

These fluffy little egg white and sugar combinations can be as varied as their more elaborate relatives, the drop and cut-out cookies. Nicknamed "kisses," meringues are often served in the Christmas season when mistletoe is a part of the decoration and the giving and receiving of a kiss from a loved one under the mistletoe is a time-honored ritual.

Folklore tells us that kissing under the mistletoe all started with a Scandinavian goddess named Frigga. Her son Balder was shot with an arrow made of a branch of mistletoe. While other goddesses attempted to save the boy, Frigga cried tears that became the white berries of the mistletoe. Frigga's friends were successful in saving Balder, and in gratitude Frigga ordered that the mistletoe should never again be used to harm anyone. Instead she made it a symbol of love and affection, and now anyone who passes under it is to be kissed.

If there is no mistletoe handy, perhaps one of the flavored puffs of sweetness will bring you a kiss of affection.

CHERRY MERINGUES

    1   cup butter or margarine
    ¾   cup sugar
    2   egg yolks
    1   cup ground walnut meats
    1¾ cups cake flour

Cream together butter and sugar, add egg yolks and beat well. Then add ground walnut meats and cake flour.

Chill until easy to handle. Form into small balls and place on greased cooky sheets.

TOPPING

2 egg whites
1 tablespoon sugar
  Candied cherries

Beat egg whites until they peak; add sugar and beat to mix. Put a dab of meringue on top of each cookie, and top with a slice of candied cherry. Bake in moderate oven (375°) about 15 minutes.

Makes about 60 cookies.

CHRISTMAS KISSES

2 egg whites
1 cup sifted sugar
⅛ teaspoon salt
1 teaspoon vinegar
1 teaspoon vanilla
½ cup finely chopped nutmeats

Beat egg whites until they are stiff and form peaks. Gradually add sugar, 2 tablespoonfuls at a time. Beat in other ingredients, except nuts. Drop batter by half teaspoonful onto lightly greased baking sheet, shaping it in cones. Bake in a very slow oven (250°) about 25 minutes, until kisses are partly dry and will hold their shape. Remove from baking sheet onto rack while hot. Decorate each kiss with nutmeats.

Makes 40 kisses.

COCOA KISSES

Increase egg whites to 3. Omit vinegar and combine vanilla with 2 teaspoons water. Add gradually half of the sugar to whipped egg whites. Add the liquid, a few drops at a time, alternating this with the remaining sugar, whipping constantly. Fold in 3 tablespoons cocoa. To bake, follow the directions for Christmas Kisses. Decorate as desired.

Makes about 46 kisses.

My daughter-in-law Kay Chambers gave this three-layered cooky recipe to me. If I want to add to its richness (which is not necessary, believe me) I use half the graham cracker mixture with the two icings, then the remaining graham cracker mixture and two additional layers of icing. (Naturally, the icing part of the recipe must then be doubled.) Be sure to use butter in this cooky.

LAYERED CHOCOLATE DREAMS

½   cup butter
¼   cup sugar
5   tablespoons cocoa
1   egg
1   cup finely shredded coconut
½   cup chopped walnuts
2   cups crushed graham crackers

Place first four ingredients in a pan over low heat. Stir until butter is melted. Add remaining ingredients and blend. Remove from heat and pour into an 8-inch-square pan, patting into an even sheet. Cover this with filling.

FILLING

¼   cup butter
3   tablespoons milk
2   tablespoons vanilla instant pudding mix
2   cups powdered sugar

Cream butter. Soak pudding in milk, stirring to blend. Add pudding mix alternately with sugar to butter. Spread evenly. Set in refrigerator for an hour or two to harden. Then add the topping.

TOPPING

1   tablespoon butter
3   squares (3 ounces) unsweetened chocolate

Melt and pour over pudding layer. Chill thoroughly before cutting into squares.

Makes 25 squares.

ANGEL COOKIES

A delicious, unbaked cooky.

¼ cup butter
¾ cup sugar
1 8-ounce package pitted dates, cut into small pieces
1 cup chopped walnuts
1 cup Rice Krispies
1 teaspoon vanilla
  Confectioners' sugar

Heat butter and sugar in a *heavy* saucepan and add dates, stirring until dates are melted. Remove from heat and cool slightly. Add walnuts, Rice Krispies, and vanilla. Form into small balls. Roll in confectioners' sugar and store in covered container until time of use.

Makes 36 cookies.

PECAN ROLLS

Another delicious cooky from the kitchen of my daughter-in-law Kay Chambers, whose children love to make this easy-to-do cooky in December or any other month.

1 cup sweet margarine
½ cup confectioners' sugar
1 tablespoon cold water
1 teaspoon vanilla or sherry
2 cups flour
⅛ teaspoon salt
2 cups chopped pecans
  Confectioners' sugar

Cream margarine and sugar and stir in water and

vanilla. Mix flour and salt and add in two additions. Stir in nutmeats. Shape into ovals about size of large dates and place on lightly greased cooky sheet. Bake in slow oven (250°) 40 minutes. Let cool slightly and roll in confectioners' sugar.

Makes 36 cookies.

Variation: divide batter into two parts and add 2 tablespoons cocoa to one part.

NÜRNBERGERS

These richly spiced and fruited honey cookies come from the famous old German city of toys and clocks.

2	eggs
1	cup honey
¾	cup light brown sugar, firmly packed
1	envelope Oetker vanillin sugar or 2 teaspoons vanilla or 1 tablespoon rum
⅛	teaspoon ground cloves
1	teaspoon cinnamon
½	teaspoon nutmeg
1	tablespoon grated lemon rind
2¾	cups flour
½	teaspoon soda
⅛	teaspoon baking powder
⅓	cup finely chopped candied citrus peel
½	cup ground unblanched almonds
½	cup hazelnuts or almonds

Beat eggs until light and frothy. Gradually add honey and sugar, beating after each addition. Stir in vanillin sugar. Sift together and stir in the spices, lemon rind, flour, soda, and baking powder. Mix in candied citrus peel and ground almonds. Cover and chill in refrigerator overnight.

Authentically, little rice-paper wafers are used as a base for the mounds. Lacking these, roll out chilled dough to a scant ¼-inch thickness. Cut into 2-inch rounds. Place one inch apart on a greased baking sheet. With fingers or the back of a spoon, round up cookies toward center to make little mounds, flattening out to edge. Press hazelnuts or almonds around the edge to give a petal effect. Bake in a hot oven (400°) about 10 minutes. Remove from oven and immediately brush with Sugar Glaze (page 159) or with Cocoa Glaze (add 1 rounded tablespoon cocoa to white glaze). Then remove at once onto wire racks to cool. Store for later use.

Makes about 6 dozen cookies.

PASTINI DI NATALE
Italian Christmas Cookies

3 cups flour
¼ teaspoon salt
3 teaspoons baking powder
1 cup softened shortening
1 cup sugar
2 eggs
1 tablespoon grated lemon rind
Lemon Glaze, colored (page 158)
¼ cup pistachio nuts

Sift together flour, salt, and baking powder. Cut in shortening until mixture has the texture of corn meal. In another bowl cream sugar and eggs. Add grated lemon rind and blend. Add to flour mixture, stirring just enough to hold ingredients together. Wrap dough in waxed paper and chill. Roll out to ¼-inch thickness on a canvas-covered or very lightly floured board. Cut into desired shapes with cooky cutters. Bake on greased cooky sheet in hot oven (425°) 8 to 10 minutes, or until golden. Remove from oven and cool. Then frost with Lemon Glaze (page 158) and decorate with pistachio nut halves.

Makes 30 cookies.

PEPPARKAKOR
Swedish Christmas Cookies

This crisp, spice-rich cooky comes from Marta Julin Nielsen, who is noted among her friends for her excellent Swedish Christmas cookies. Mrs. Nielsen reminds us that the animal cut-out is used a great deal in Sweden—particularly the pig, which signifies good fortune.

    1   cup butter or margarine
    1½ cups sugar
    3   tablespoons light corn syrup
    2   eggs

3   cups flour (approximately)
½   teaspoon soda
½   teaspoon salt
1   teaspoon cinnamon
½   teaspoon ground ginger
½   teaspoon allspice
¼   teaspoon ground cloves

Cream the butter and sugar. Add the syrup and eggs. Sift together dry ingredients and add to butter-egg mixture. Work into a stiff dough. Wrap in waxed paper and refrigerate at least two hours. Roll quite thin on a floured board. Cut with cooky cutter in shape of star, Christmas tree, animal, bell, etc. Bake about 10 minutes in a moderate oven (350°).

Makes about sixty 2½-inch cookies.

If cloves give the greatest potpourri of scent, pepper is the most pungent of all spices. It adds a gourmet touch to mincemeat, some cookies, tartlets, and other Christmas delicacies.

White pepper is less pungent than black and is not as popular in the United States as black pepper, but it is enjoying expanding use as American cooks come to appreciate it for bread stuffings and poultry flavoring, soups, meats, eggs, pickling, and a host of other foods, where its subtle flavor gives zest. *Pfeffernüsse* are an old German Christmas cooky, and these distinctive "Pepper Nuts" have become a traditional favorite for holiday feasting in this country too.

Almost every woman who bakes Christmas cookies has her favorite *Pfeffernüsse* cooky recipe, and I am no exception. I am indebted to my good friend Virginia Nielsen McCall, author of books for young readers, for this recipe, which I find superlative.

PFEFFERNÜSSE
German Pepper Nuts

½   cup sugar
½   cup butter or margarine
½   cup light corn syrup
1   tablespoon molasses
½   cup coffee
1¼ teaspoons anise seed
2   eggs
3¼ cups flour
1½ teaspoon soda
¼   teaspoon cinnamon
⅛   teaspoon white pepper
½   teaspoon freshly grated nutmeg
⅛   teaspoon salt
½   cup mixed candied fruits, chopped very fine
½   cup pecans, chopped very fine

Combine sugar, butter, corn syrup, molasses, and coffee
and simmer 5 minutes. Add anise seed. Remove from heat
and cool. Beat in eggs. Sift together flour, soda, spices,
and salt. Blend into liquid mixture. Stir vigorously. Add
candied fruit (must be chopped or minced very small) and
stir. Add nutmeats and stir again to blend completely.
Wrap in waxed paper and chill in refrigerator overnight.

Roll into small balls and place on baking sheet, spacing
2 inches apart. Bake in preheated moderate oven (350°)
15 to 18 minutes. While hot, dip top of cookies in Glaze.
Drain on waxed paper until glaze is dry.

Makes about 6 dozen 1-inch balls.

GLAZE

1 cup sugar
½ cup water
½ teaspoon cream of tartar
⅓ cup (or more) confectioners' sugar

Combine first three ingredients and bring to a boil. Add sugar and stir to blend, cooking about 1 minute.

SCANDINAVIAN DROPS

Somewhat like the Swedish jam "biscuits" known as *Dubbla Syltkakor*, these little drop cookies are quick to make, delicate in taste with the addition of your favorite jelly.

½ cup unsalted margarine
¼ cup light brown sugar, firmly packed
1 egg, separated
1 cup sifted flour
¾ cup ground or grated almonds
   Tart jelly

Cream margarine, blend in sugar, add egg yolk, and beat until light. Blend in flour, and roll dough into small balls 1 inch in diameter. Beat egg white slightly with fork. Dip cookies in egg white, then roll them in chopped nuts and place on a greased cooky sheet, making a depression in center of each cooky. Bake 5 minutes in a slow oven (300°). Remove and press down centers again. Continue baking for 30 to 35 minutes. Remove to wire rack. When slightly cooled, fill centers with jelly, candied cherry, or small pieces of candied apricot or prune.

Makes 24 cookies.

CHRISTMAS SNOWBALLS

My cousin Mrs. Russell Smith of Woodbury, Connecticut, makes delicious Christmas Snowballs for the holidays. Appropriate to serve in homes where gardens may be powdered with December snow, they are equally tasty in California or Florida in May or December.

- 1 cup sifted flour
- 2 tablespoons sugar
- ¼ teaspoon salt
- ½ cup butter or margarine
- 1 tablespoon rum
- 1 cup chopped pecans
  Confectioners' sugar

Sift flour. Mix sugar, salt, and butter together. Work in the rum, nutmeats, and flour. Mixture will be very thick. Form into small balls (½ inch) and bake on an ungreased cooky sheet for 20 minutes or more in a slow oven (325°). Remove to wire rack. While still hot, dip in confectioners' sugar. When cool, roll again in sugar. Store in covered container.

Makes 24 to 30 balls.

HOLIDAY RUM BALLS

- 3 cups vanilla cooky or graham cracker crumbs
- 3 tablespoons cocoa
- 1½ cups sifted confectioners' sugar
- ⅛ teaspoon salt

1¼ cups finely chopped nutmeats (pecans are excellent)
⅓ cup rum or whisky, or 2 teaspoons vanilla
2   tablespoons honey or molasses
½ cup or more confectioners' sugar

Combine finely ground vanilla cooky crumbs in a large mixing bowl with cocoa, sifted confectioners' sugar, salt, and nutmeats, stirring to blend. Mix flavoring with honey or molasses and add liquid ingredients slowly to the crumb mixture, using hands to gauge proper consistency. When the ingredients hold together without breaking, stop adding liquid. If mixture should seem to be too dry, add a few more drops of liquid. Form into 1-inch balls. Roll them in powdered sugar and store for at least two days to ripen before serving.

Makes about 60 balls.

SPEKULATIUS
German Spice Cookies

The recipe for this traditional Christmas favorite was brought from Germany by Petra Wertz.

4   cups sifted flour
2   teaspoons baking powder or 1 package Oetker Backin
1   cup sugar
½ teaspoon ground coriander
1   teaspoon cinnamon
1   teaspoon ground cloves
½ teaspoon nutmeg
¼ teaspoon cardamom
1   egg
1   envelope Oetker vanillin sugar or 2 teaspoons vanilla
3   tablespoons milk
¾ cup margarine
½ cup ground almonds or hazelnuts

Sift the flour and baking powder into a mixing bowl. Make a well in center, and add sugar, spices, egg, vanillin sugar or vanilla, and milk. Work together, from outside in, to form a heavy paste. Dice margarine and add it with nuts to the paste. Stir to blend. Add more flour if necessary to make a manageable dough. Make into a ball and chill in refrigerator at least two hours. Turn onto a lightly floured board and roll to about ⅛-inch thickness. Cut into fancy shapes of animals, stars, circles, and figures. Place on a greased cooky sheet, and bake in a hot oven (400°) for 7 to 8 minutes. Cool on wire racks.

Makes about 5 dozen cookies.

Note: These are somewhat similar to the Danish *Brune Kager* and the Dutch *Speculaas*, the Santa Claus cakes of these countries, without which no Christmas season would be complete. The Danish version shapes the dough into a loaf, wraps it in waxed paper and allows it to stand overnight before slicing it for baking. The Dutch version is a soft cooky which is cut into squares.

SPRINGERLE
"Picture" Cookies

This beautiful Christmas cooky is one of the treasures of Central European Christmas cookies, but belongs no less to the Pennsylvania Dutch whose ancestors arrived on America's shores with recipes and *Springerle* boards from their native land. The dough is very firm, and designs are imprinted on it from wooden forms. These molds are square or rectangular in shape and usually have handles. The boards are marked off in squares which make beautiful "cameos" or pictures of leaping animals, flowers, fruits, dancing figures, Christmas symbols, castles with turrets, to mention a few.

This cooky is tricky to make and is not recommended for the beginner. Each little picture is framed in a square, which some writers think refers to *Springer,* a German noun for knight in the game of chess, or as a verb meaning to leap or jump. The mold pictures are thus related symbolically to the pastimes of kings.

Like the Italian *Biscotti,* the Springerle is known as a dunking cooky. The use of anise and lemon makes the flavor of the cooky as special as its carving. Less traditional, but often used, is additional melted butter to increase softness. Miss Anna Marie Nadolny, who grew up in Switzerland, advises dampening bottom of each cooky with a little sugar water, and placing the cookies in a tightly covered tin for 2 weeks to allow to "ripen." After a few days put an apple in tin but do not allow to spoil.

2   large eggs
⅞   cup sifted confectioners' sugar
1   envelope Oetker vanillin sugar or 2 teaspoons vanilla plus 1 tablespoon confectioners' sugar
1   cup plus 2 tablespoons flour
⅛   teaspoon baking powder
2   tablespoons anise seed

Whip the eggs with a heavy wire whisk or beat at high speed with an electric mixer. Gradually add sugar and continue to beat until mixture is thick and foamy. Combine vanillin sugar, flour, and baking powder, and sift into egg mixture, using as much flour as is needed to make a very firm dough. Turn out dough onto a pastry board lightly sprinkled with flour and knead until it becomes smooth and free of all stickiness. Add extra flour if necessary at this point. Chill dough in refrigerator for at least two hours.

Turn dough onto lightly floured board and roll out to about ⅜-inch thickness. Flour *Springerle* board and press it firmly into dough to get a good print. Separate the forms into squares, circles, or rectangles and place them on a lightly greased cooky sheet sprinkled with anise seed. Allow them to stand for 24 hours to dry out. Then bake in a slow oven (275°) 30 to 35 minutes. Remove to racks and allow to stand overnight to "soften" before storing.

Makes about 24 molded cookies.

SPRITSAR
Spritz Rings

A traditional Swedish cooky as made by the Swedish American Steamship Line.

1 cup butter
½ cup sugar
1 egg yolk
6 blanched bitter almonds, grated
2½ cups flour

Work butter and sugar until creamy and fluffy. Add egg yolk, almonds, and flour and mix thoroughly. Shape in rings or S's with cooky press. Place on buttered baking sheet and bake in moderate oven (350°) until golden yellow, about 8 minutes.

Makes 40 to 50 cookies.

SWEDISH ALMOND COOKIES

1 cup (½ pound) softened butter or margarine
1 cup sugar
1 egg

1   cup finely ground almonds
2   cups flour
1   teaspoon salt
¼   teaspoon almond extract

Cream the butter until light and fluffy. Gradually beat in the sugar and egg. Stir in almonds. Sift flour, measure, and sift with the salt. Stir into creamed mixture. Add the almond extract. Shape into small balls, the size of walnuts. Place on ungreased baking sheet. Flatten each ball with back of spoon. Bake in a moderate oven (350°) 10 to 15 minutes, or until golden brown. Allow to cool on wire rack before storing.

Makes 72 cookies.

SWISS CHRISTMAS COOKIES

Three generations of use in Adele Matthias Nederburgh's family recommends the excellent recipe which follows. As a little girl Mrs. Nederburgh made both the chocolate and white cookies with her mother, Virginie Matthias Booker; now her own boys mix the doughs with her in their California kitchen for Christmas (and other) use.

5   egg whites
4   cups (4 pounds) almonds, finely ground
2   cups sugar
1   cup ground unsweetened chocolate
1   teaspoon cinnamon
1   teaspoon allspice

Beat egg whites until very stiff. Mix remaining ingredients together until thoroughly blended. Then fold in egg
whites, gently blending. Roll out to ¼-inch thickness in
granulated sugar instead of flour. Cut with shaped cutters.
(Lucky you if you happen to have any of the beautiful
Swiss ones.) Bake in a preheated slow oven (300°) on well-
greased cooky sheets about 8 minutes. Do not overbake,
as cookies will darken.

Makes about ninety-six 1-inch circles or forty-six 2¼-
inch stars.

During Christmas holidays every Austrian home offers
plates stacked with small and dainty cookies, and most of
them are named with diminutives, as *Kipferln, Krapferln,*
and *Plätzchen.*

VANILLEKIPFERLN
Vanilla Crescents

¾   cup butter or margarine
⅓   cup sugar
2   cups flour
1½   cups blanched almonds, finely chopped
1   envelope Oetker vanillin sugar or 3 tablespoons
    vanilla sugar

Store 3 tablespoons sugar overnight or longer in a tightly closed jar with a vanilla bean if you can't get Oetker
vanillin sugar. Cream butter and ⅓ cup sugar, add flour

and almonds and work into a dough with hands. Pinch off dough and form small crescents about 2 inches long. Place on an ungreased cooky sheet and bake in a preheated slow oven (275°) 15 to 20 minutes. Roll crescents in vanilla sugar while hot. Cool on racks.

Makes 36 crescents.

CHRISTMAS WALNUT SQUARES

- ½ cup margarine
- 1 cup sugar
- 2 eggs, well beaten
- 1½ cups flour
- ½ teaspoon baking powder
- 1½ teaspoons sherry

Cream margarine until lemon yellow; add sugar and continue creaming until fluffy. Add eggs, flour, baking powder, and sherry. Spread mixture in a lightly oiled 13 × 15-inch jelly roll pan. Cover with topping.

TOPPING

- 2 egg whites, stiffly beaten
- 1 cup light brown sugar
- ¼ cup walnuts, chopped small
- ⅓ cup drained maraschino cherries, cut up

Beat egg whites until stiff. Fold in brown sugar, nutmeats, and maraschino cherries. Spread over cooky dough.

Bake in preheated moderate oven (350°) 20 to 25 minutes. Cut into squares while warm, but not hot.

Makes 48 squares.

Cinnamon is said to have a thousand uses. Certainly it is worked hard in scenting Christmas foods, as it is a favorite in hot spiced drinks, as well as in many pies, coffeecakes, sweet breads, puddings, and cookies. German Cinnamon Stars are a mouth-watering sample of the use of this fragrant spice.

ZIMTSTERNE
German Cinnamon Stars

5   medium egg whites
2   cups sifted light brown sugar
⅛   teaspoon salt
1   teaspoon cinnamon
3   cups grated, not ground, unblanched almonds
1½ cups confectioners' sugar

Beat egg whites until stiff. Gradually add brown sugar and salt and continue to beat until blended thoroughly, so that mixture retains mark of a knife blade. Put aside ¼ cup of this mixture for frosting. Add cinnamon and grated almonds to egg white and sugar mixture and stir in enough confectioners' sugar to make a stiff dough. Turn out onto board sprinkled with confectioners' sugar or onto a pastry canvas and knead lightly to mold all together.

Form into a ball and wrap in waxed paper and refrigerate overnight for easy handling. Working with a small amount at a time, pat or roll out to ⅛-inch thickness on board covered with a pastry canvas or a sprinkling of confectioners' sugar. Cut with a star cutter dipped in confectioners' sugar. Place each cut-out on greased cooky sheet. Frost tops with egg white-sugar mixture reserved for this purpose. Bake in a slow oven (325°) for 15 to 25 minutes or until "dry." Remove and cool for storage or use.

Makes 2 dozen or more 1½-inch stars.

Note: Confectioners' sugar may be substituted for brown sugar for another version of *Zimtsterne*.

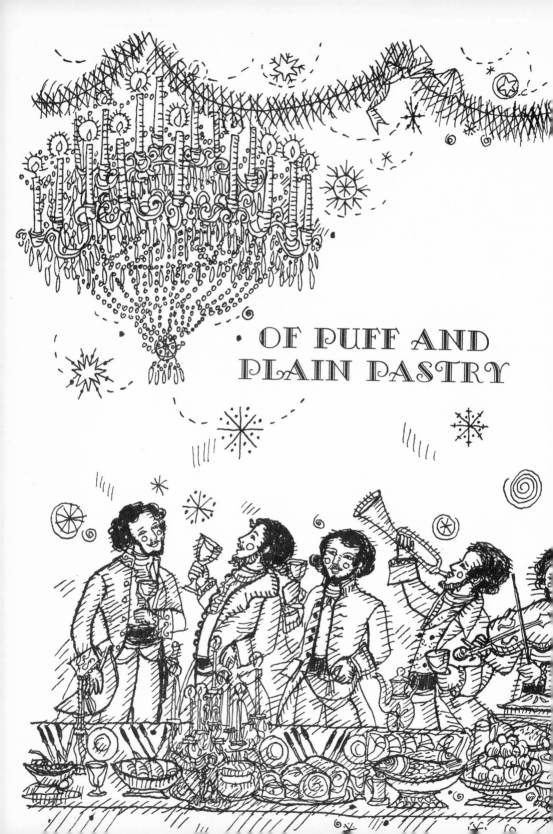

OF PUFF AND PLAIN PASTRY

PASTRY SECRETS

A S IN ALL baking, before you begin to make pastry be sure to read through the recipe, assemble ingredients and utensils, and follow directions exactly.

Sift flour before measuring it.

Preheat oven to required temperature.

Remember that too much flour will make pie crust tough.

Too much shortening produces a dry and crumbly crust.

Too much liquid produces a heavy and soggy crust.

For best results be sure that all ingredients and utensils are cold.

For a well-baked, brown lower crust, choose pie pan of heat-resistant glass or enamelware. A shiny metal surface will not give you desired results because it deflects heat rather than absorbing it. If you want to use a tin pan, "season" it until its shininess has worn off. If aluminum is your choice, be sure to choose a pan of satiny finish.

Handle dough as little as possible in mixing and shaping. Cut the shortening into sifted flour with two knives or with a pastry blender.

Add shortening in two additions, being sure to cut in first addition until mixture is very fine, like corn meal. This makes for a tender crust. Cut in remaining shortening until lumps are the size of a pea. This will give flakiness to your crust.

Although the experts tell us it is not necessary to chill dough when ice water is used, I do chill any dough and even keep one half chilled while working with other half.

For best results, use a cloth-covered rolling pin and turn dough onto a lightly floured, cloth-covered board.

Roll dough in only one direction, never back and forth.

Roll dough for top crust a little thinner than for bottom crust, and allow it to extend 1 inch beyond edge of pan for proper turning under, sealing, and crimping.

To prevent edge of crust from becoming too brown, band with a wet strip to be removed after baking. Plan on 6 servings from an 8-inch pie; 7 to 8 servings from a 9-inch pie.

Pie Crusts

REGULAR or fancy, pie shells and crusts often make the difference between a good pie and an excellent one. Here are some recipes for standard pastry and modern combination mixes to make your December pastries that something special to set off your choice fillings.

PLAIN PASTRY

Some excellent pastry cooks insist that lard must be used to ensure quality pastry. Others, and I am one, think you can have a very acceptable product with vegetable shortening, oil, or margarine as the fat. First let's look at an old traditional recipe.

For 9-inch Pie	For 8-inch Pie
2 cups sifted flour	1½ cups sifted flour
1 teaspoon salt	¾ teaspoon salt
⅔ cup lard or ⅝ cup vegetable shortening (if hydrogenated, add 1 more tablespoon shortening)	½ cup lard or ½ cup plus 1 tablespoon vegetable shortening
4 tablespoons ice water*	3 tablespoons ice water*

Mix together sifted flour and salt. Cut in one half of shortening until mixture is the texture of corn meal. Cut in the other half coarsely until particles are about the size of a pea. Sprinkle with water, 1 tablespoon at a time, and mix lightly with a fork. Lift fork high to bring air into mixture and to keep pastry tender. Do not overdo. Add just enough water to make ingredients adhere together. Then press dough *lightly* with hands into a ball. Wrap in waxed paper and chill while preparing filling (or longer).

Divide dough, returning one ball to refrigerator until ready to use. Place on lightly floured cloth-covered board. Flatten dough with hand to about ¼ inch. Work lightly

---

*In fruit juice pastry such as orange, lemon, etc., simply use desired *chilled* fruit juice in place of water. For nut pastry for holiday custard or chiffon pies, add ¼ cup ground nuts to flour. For cheese pastry, add ¾ cup grated cheddar cheese to flour.

as you roll out dough to about ⅛-inch thickness. Keep rounding edges of pastry, piecing together if breaks develop and keeping pastry circular. Roll out so that dough is about 1 inch larger than pan to allow for depth. Fold pastry in half and place in pan. Unfold, and pat into shape without stretching it. Trim off any overhanging edges. Brush inside of bottom crust with egg white if desired. Add filling. Roll out remaining dough for top crust a little thinner than for bottom crust so that 1 inch extends beyond pie pan. Fold in half, and make slits to allow for steam to escape. Moisten edge of bottom crust with water. Add filling. Fit dough for top crust over filling. Unfold. Trim if necessary, allowing ½ inch for turn under. Fold the extra edge of top pastry under edge of lower pastry. Seal by pressing against edge of pan. Flute or form crimp with forefinger of right and left hand or with thumb and forefinger. For interwoven lattice tops for fruit pies, cut ½-inch strips of pastry with a pastry wheel, weave crisscross on waxed paper, chill, and flip quickly over top of filling. Seal and finish edges of pie. For baking time, see each recipe.

Makes one 2-crust pie.

EASY FLAKY PASTRY

To make Flaky Pastry for a one-crust pie, roll half of Plain Pastry ⅛ inch thick, and dot bits of firm butter or margarine (1 tablespoon per crust) over surface of circle. Fold so two sides meet in center, and seal by pressing edges together with fingers. Fold ends to center and seal. Roll out, and fit into pie plate. Prick pastry to prevent puffing during baking. If it puffs up anyway, quickly prick again in two places. Bake in preheated very hot oven (475°) for 8 minutes. Cool and fill with desired filling or follow directions of individual recipe.

FRENCH SHORT CRUST PASTRY

The French have a way with pastry. One of their tricks is to let it "rest" for 12 to 24 hours before use. This resting period makes it easier to work with and the pastry takes on less color when baking.

    ¾   cup margarine
    1½ cups flour
    ½   teaspoon salt
    2   to 3 tablespoons ice water or cold milk

Cut margarine into flour with two knives until mixture is in lumps about the size of peas. Be sure each piece of fat is coated with flour but is *not too small.* Add just enough water to moisten.

Makes one 10-inch pie crust.

VEGETABLE OIL PASTRY

A new way to use vegetable oil for flaky pie crust.

    2   cups flour
    ½   teaspoon salt
    ½   cup vegetable oil, frozen
    ¼   cup nonfat milk

Mix flour and salt. Cut in frozen oil as in regular pastry making, working fast. Stir in very cold milk. Pat gently into a ball and roll between two sheets of waxed paper. If pastry tears in shaping in pie plate, just press it together. Cut circle for lower crust at least 1 inch larger than top one so edges can cover top edge and seal all together. Fill and bake as specified in recipe.

Makes one 2-crust pie.

COOKY CRUST

20 sugar-cooky crumbs
½ cup softened margarine
½ teaspoon vanilla or almond extract

Combine ingredients. Pour into a 9-inch pie plate. Press crumbs firmly against bottom and sides of pie plate. Chill. Another good base for "cream" or chiffon pies.

Note: ½ cup finely ground almonds may be added to Cooky Crust when a distinct almond flavor is desired.

Chocolate cookies may be substituted for sugar cooky crumbs when a chocolate flavor is desired.

Makes one 9-inch pie crust.

GRAHAM CRACKER CRUST

1¼ cups graham cracker crumbs
¼ cups softened margarine
¼ cup sugar

Combine graham cracker crumbs with margarine and sugar. Pour into a 9-inch pie plate. Press crumbs firmly against bottom and sides of pie plate. Bake in a moderate oven (375°) 8 minutes. Cool.

Makes one 9-inch pie crust.

SANKA-COCONUT SHELL

1 can (3½ ounces) shredded coconut
  Double strength Sanka or coffee
2 tablespoons margarine

Empty can of coconut into a bowl. Add enough Sanka to barely cover. Let stand 5 minutes. Drain. Turn out onto double-thick paper towels. Rub margarine on bottom and sides of 9-inch pan and press coconut on "buttered" pie plate. Bake in a moderate oven (350°) 10 minutes. Cool.

Makes one 9-inch pie crust.

WALNUT-GINGER CRUST

A delicious crust for eggnog or custard fillings.

½   cup ground walnut meats
¾   cup crushed gingersnap crumbs
2   tablespoons sugar
¼   cup softened margarine

Combine all ingredients and mix thoroughly. Press firmly against bottom and sides of 9-inch pie plate. Bake in a moderate oven (350°) 8 minutes. Cool.

Makes one 9-inch pie crust.

Before Mince Pies

IN ENGLAND, it is said, Christmas Day is celebrated gastronomically with greater splendor than in France. Alfred Suzanne wrote in *La Cuisine anglaise et américaine* that the English celebration of Christmas is memorable apart from its religious significance "because it evokes great slaughter of turkeys, geese, and all kinds of game, a wholesale massacre of fat oxen, pigs, and sheep, they envisage garlands of black puddings, sausages and saveloys . . . mountains of plum puddings and oven-fulls of mince pies."

In Elizabethan days a huge mince pie was kept on a table throughout the Christmas season—an invitation to guests to "cut and come again."

Preparation was long and arduous, if we are to believe Samuel Pepys who wrote in his *Diary* (1666) that on Christmas Day he arose late "leaving my wife desirous to sleep, having sat up till four this morning seeing her mayds make mince pies."

The absence of mince pies from the English Christmas dinner would be looked upon as "a breach of the traditional rules and customs." Yet it was not always so. In Oliver Cromwell's time, when mince pies were known also as "Christmas pies," the Puritans condemned them "as a hodge-podge of superstition and would have none of them." For more than a hundred years ministers of the gospel argued for or against the serving of "minc'd pies."

In the time before the Reformation, mince pies were made oblong in shape to represent the manger. Sometimes a little figure of the infant Jesus would be placed in an indentation on the top crust. Thus the pie was served as an object of devotion as well as a part of the feast. The "baby" was removed, and the "manger" was eaten.

This custom was suppressed by the Puritans, who thought it was unreligious to eat the pastry manger. Thenceforth the mince pie appeared in its present circular shape. But the idea of the small, individual pie persisted. A belief developed that you must eat a mince pie of tartlet size every day between Christmas Day and Twelfth Night if you wanted to be sure of good luck in the twelve months to come.

In America, when the Puritans in New England tried to make Thanksgiving take the place of Christmas and almost succeeded for a time, they also transferred the English Christmas dinner of a bird and a mince pie to their new feast day. The South would have none of it. Their Christmas dinners reflected their pride in their English heritage of goods and social customs, and featured "mince meat flavored vigorously enough to make one's head swim."

And so mince pie came to stay. With the passage of time, however, its ingredients were altered to decrease or even eliminate the amount of meat used. The fruit version is strictly American, and of course Little Jack Horner's

Christmas pie was our American mince pie. The "plum" he pulled out from its savory depths was a big, fat raisin.

Whether you like your mince pie chock-full of meat or a mélange of spiced fruits, serve it forth with pride in its rich history.

Come let us like our jovial sires of old
With gambols and mince pies our Christmas hold.

MINCEMEAT

The tongue gives this mincemeat its special flavor. I like to use at least as much apple by measurement as meat mixture. Other cooks prefer a two to one ratio. Let your own preferences guide you.

1½ pounds lean chuck
½ pound fresh beef tongue
½ pound chopped suet
1 package (15 ounces) seeded raisins, cut small
1 cup seedless raisins
½ cup citron, diced small
1 cup brown sugar, firmly packed
½ cup unsulfured molasses
1 cup sugar
½ cup orange marmalade
2 teaspoons salt
½ nutmeg, ground
1½ teaspoons cinnamon
1½ teaspoons allspice
½ teaspoon ground cloves
½ teaspoon mace
1 teaspoon pepper
  Meat stock
6 to 8 or more tart apples, peeled and chopped fine
1 cup or more brandy

Mix together cooked and finely diced beef and tongue. Stir in chopped suet, cut-up raisins and whole seedless raisins, citron, brown sugar, molasses, sugar, marmalade, salt, and seasonings. Cover with the stock in which meats were boiled, mixing well. Bring to a boil over low heat. Then add apples. Simmer mixture for 1 hour, stirring frequently. Add brandy, and correct for flavor. You must taste this to be sure spices and brandy are in amounts wanted for the special flavor you want to achieve. Pour into sterilized jars and seal or freeze for at least one month for flavors to mellow.

Makes 6 large pies.

LEMON MINCEMEAT

2   large lemons
1   pound tart apples, chopped
½   pound suet, chopped fine
2   cups currants
1   cup seeded raisins, chopped
1   cup seedless raisins
2   cups sugar
⅓   cup candied lemon peel slices
2   tablespoons citron
1   tablespoon or more mixed spices, including allspice, cinnamon, and nutmeg to taste
¼   cup brandy or rum

Pare the lemons, squeeze them, and reserve the juice. Boil the peel until tender enough to mash—put into the blender for this if you have one. Add apples to mashed lemon, then add suet, currants, raisins, sugar, candied lemon peel, citron, and spices. Strain lemon juice into these ingredients and blend. Spoon this into a sterilized jar, allowing ½ inch space at top. Add brandy or rum and cover with close-fitting lid. Refrigerate. Stir occasionally, and in not less than 10 days use as desired.

Makes about 4 to 5 pounds of mincemeat.

GREEN TOMATO MINCEMEAT

4 quarts (16 cups) green tomatoes
2 quarts (8 cups) tart apples
¼ pound (1 cup) suet (optional)
3 cups light brown sugar, firmly packed
1 teaspoon allspice
2 teaspoons cinnamon
½ teaspoon ground cloves
1 teaspoon nutmeg
6 cups seedless raisins
⅓ cup cider vinegar

Chop in blender, or in small quantities by hand, tomatoes, apples, and suet. Put into a large stewing pan. Add remaining ingredients. Simmer at low heat until tender (at least 2 hours). Bottle in hot sterilized jars and store for later use. Allow 1 pint per 8-inch pie (will serve six).

Makes 10 pints.

Apple Pie for Breakfast

Oh! flakey and crust succulent pie,
They call you dyspeptic, 'tis hereso, fie!
—Source unknown

IF YOU THINK of apple pie only as a special-occasion dessert, you are in for a surprise. As recently as 1902 an English "Culinary Guide" suggested serving apple pie only twice a week. The repercussions from American housewives and newspaper articles were as loud as though the red-coated British troops had fired on Bunker Hill once again.

The *New York Times* commented that this allowance was "utterly insufficient, as anyone who knows the secret of the strength of your nation must admit. Pie is the American synonym of prosperity, and its varying contents the calendar of changing seasons. Pie is the food of the heroic. No pie-eating people can ever be permanently vanquished."

Apple pie was a staple in colonial days. Whatever else the breakfast might contain, it was certain to include buckwheat cakes and apple pie. A man had to have his pie to do the morning's work. Then there would be apple pie to look forward to at the noontime dinner, perhaps again for supper.

In many homes as many as seven different kinds of pie were served, and apple pie was sure to be one of them. Pie was not served, however, in the earliest years of colonial living, for flour and sugar were then in scarce supply. Loaf sugar was saved for guests, flour to make special breads when the minister came to dine.

In the formative years of our history, Dutch farmhouses of New York and Pennsylvania had their great bins of apples which were stored alongside turnips, beets, and other root vegetables. In Orange County, New York, and elsewhere it was customary for neighbors to gather in October to peel, quarter, and core ripe pippins and greenings while doing a little socializing. Often a young woman met her mate at one of these affairs, for in the evening after the farm work was completed, the men gathered too and eating and dancing culminated a busy day.

As the frontier moved westward John Chapman, known in folklore as Johnny Appleseed, carried apple seeds into the areas between the Alleghenies and the Mississippi Valley to start vast new orchard lands. In time he became more famous as a legendary character than William Blaxton, a farmer-clergyman who moved from his Boston farm to Rhode Island in 1635 and there raised what is now called the Rhode Island greening—the first apple, as a distinct type, to be grown in America.

From these apples and others that followed, apple pies came to be made in three ways: open-faced, latticed, and with a covered top. A piece of cheese was sure to be served with the pie!

In 1758 a Swedish pastor named Dr. Israel Acrelius wrote home: "Apple-pie is used through the whole year, and when fresh apples are no longer to be had, dried ones are used. It is the evening meal of children. House-pie, in country places, is made of apples neither peeled nor freed from their cores, and its crust is not broken if a wagon wheel goes over it."

In my own childhood, my Maine-born grandmother Palmer often served a thick hearty soup with wedges of apple pie and cheese for Saturday breakfast. It was a wonderfully satisfying choice, and the pie vanished like the early morning dew in summer. I have always been grateful to Grandma for introducing me to variations in breakfast menus, and apple pie was one of the best. I am glad too that in my childhood apple pie was not restricted to an occasional evening meal and for Christmas feasting, for I think it was in those years that my taste buds were beginning to become quite food-conscious.

In Grandma's nineteenth-century childhood, apples were peeled, quartered, strung on cords, and draped, along with peppers and pumpkins, around her mother's kitchen in Bangor, as they had been in her grandmother's time. There they remained until they dried and their spicy richness permeated the big kitchen with a promise of fragrant pies to come. In those times dried-apple pies in winter months were considered a real treat.

Across the Atlantic in the Bedfordshire area of England the apple pie came to be known as "Apple Florentine." It was as much an indispensable part of the Christmas feast as orange jelly, mince pie, and plum pudding were and still are in other areas. Apple Florentine was a very large pie and was served either in its cooking container or in a deep pewter, Sheffield, or even gold dish or casserole. The Florentine was made of "good cooking apples," sugar, and lemon, and had a "covering" of rich pastry. When this was baked and just before serving, the crust was lifted off and cut into triangular pieces. A full quart of hissing-hot ale was poured over the fruit, and the little triangles were then arranged in place.

MARK TWAIN'S MUSH APPLE PIE

Mark Twain is known to most of us as a humorist. But he was also something of an observer of food customs, and he had his own idea of what an apple pie should be.

He believed that an unbaked pastry shell should be filled with cold applesauce made of greening apples, sweetened to taste, and rubbed through a sieve to a mush. The fruit was topped with thinly rolled pastry, slashed for venting, and carefully sealed around the edges. This was baked in a preheated hot oven (450°) 20 minutes, then cooked about 20 minutes longer at 375° until crust was golden brown.

APPLE PIE WITH CHEESE PASTRY

> But I, when I undress me
> Each night, upon my knees
> Will ask the Lord to bless me
> With apple-pie and cheese.
> —EUGENE FIELD, "Apple-Pie and Cheese"

Cheese Pastry (page 204)
¾ cup sugar
1 tablespoon flour
1 teaspoon, or less, caraway seeds (or cinnamon)
⅛ teaspoon salt
2 tablespoons vinegar
3 drops Angostura bitters
4 to 6 greenings or other tart apples, peeled, cored, and sliced thin
1 tablespoon margarine
   Milk
   Sugar

Line 8-inch pie plate with pastry. Mix sugar, flour,

caraway seeds, salt, vinegar, and Angostura bitters. Slice apples into this mixture. Arrange row of apples inside shell about ½ inch from edge and work toward center until shell is covered and apples mound slightly toward center. Dot with margarine, and wet edges of under crust. Cover with upper crust and seal edges securely by crimping. Prick or slash upper crust in several places. Bake in a pre-heated hot oven (425°) 45 to 55 minutes.

Ten minutes before pie has finished baking, brush top lightly with milk and sprinkle with sugar.

Makes one 8-inch pie.

Note: One tablespoon lemon juice and the grated rind of 1 lemon may be substituted for vinegar to point up flavor. And you may flavor to suit. (The caraway flavor is excellent.)

REDWOOD ROOM APPLE PIE

The Redwood Room at the Clift Hotel in San Francisco is noted for its excellent cuisine and restaurant service. One of its famous specialties is its Apple Pie with a unique topping, as originated by Chief Chef Ove Anderson. You are apt to forget all about the handsome panels of 2000-year-old curly redwood and the silver-leaf ceiling with blond wood inlays once the pastry cart comes your way.

Your choice? Apple Pie, of course, since it is a specialty of the Redwood Room and a perfect pie for a December dinner. Easy to prepare, this apple pie with its special topping can be featured in your December entertaining and increase your reputation as a gourmet cook.

1   tablespoon cornstarch
½   cup sugar
¼   cup heavy cream
3   tablespoons butter
1   tablespoon lemon juice
1   1-pound, 4-ounce can pie-sliced apples, drained
1   9-inch baked pastry shell

Combine cornstarch and sugar in saucepan; stir in cream, mixing well. Cook over medium heat until boiling; stir in butter and lemon juice. Add drained apples and simmer for 10 minutes, stirring occasionally. Cool. Then spoon into baked crust, filling shell ¾ full.

TOPPING

1   8-ounce package cream cheese
⅓   cup sugar
1   egg
½   cup grated coconut
½   cup chopped walnut meats

Beat cream cheese and sugar until fluffy; beat in egg. Spoon over apple filling. Sprinkle coconut and walnut meats over top. Bake in preheated moderate oven (350°) for 15 to 20 minutes or until topping is golden brown. Cool before serving.

Makes one 9-inch pie.

CHESS PIE

This is another of Dr. Helen Christensen's excellent recipes that is good any time of the year, but is especially suited to December use because of its nut-raisin richness. An old-time favorite, it is a blue-ribbon winner with men, and is easy for even the beginning cook to prepare.

½   cup softened butter or margarine
1½ cups sugar
4   eggs, beaten
¼   teaspoon salt
2   teaspoons vanilla
6   tablespoons milk
1   cup mixed nuts, chopped
1   cup raisins
1   9-inch unbaked pastry shell

Cream butter and gradually add sugar. Add well-beaten eggs and stir to blend. Beat in salt, vanilla, and milk. Stir in nuts and raisins, mixing thoroughly. Pour into prepared pastry shell. Bake in preheated hot oven (450°) 10 minutes. Reduce heat to 350° and continue baking for 30 minutes. The filling will appear soft when removed from oven but will become firm. Garnish with nut halves or sour cream, if desired.

Makes one 9-inch pie—at least 8 servings (because of richness).

In the garden islands of the Pacific—the tropical Hawaiian Islands—May-in-December weather invites a happy, joyful celebration of Christmas. Christmas Eve and Christmas Day are brightened by pageantry at Islam Palace in Honolulu, the only royal palace on American soil, and by fireworks that make the night as colorful as the day.

Laughter, friendliness, and leis are all a part of the big island celebration, as anyone who has ever taken a Christmas cruise to Honolulu will tell you,

Christmas visitors are welcomed with leis, Hawaiian style, in a custom introduced by Pete Fithian many years ago. The rest is up to the visitor, for hospitality reigns supreme on this island where orchids grow wild and the ginger, poinsettias, and pikake scent the air with as much fragrance as baking does in island kitchens.

Whether you want to indulge in tropical fruits such as papaya, mango, or passion fruit at Don the Beachcomber's or at the Royal Hawaiian Hotel, feast on fried or poached *mahi mahi* (a delicate white fish of superb flavor) at the Outrigger Club, or eat one of the luscious fruit pies that has helped to make famous the cuisine of Hana Maui Hotel on the neighboring island of Maui, you are in for some delectable dining. Of course you can have all of the traditional foods of the Continental U.S.A., if you must.

Christmas first came to these islands in 1786 when Captain George Dixon and his English crew thought about Christmas in their native land—the glistening mistletoe and holly, the rich pies, cakes, and plum puddings of other Christmases. Still, they were sailors and could feel at home in any port.

Captain Dixon was a practical man and ordered a pig to be brought from shore, and other "trimmings" for the special dinner. The Christmas Day ration of grog was mixed with the juice of coconuts as the men toasted family and friends in faraway England from the deck of the *Charlotte* in Waimea Bay, Kauai, Sandwich Islands (later named Hawaiian Islands).

On a nearby ship was Captain Nathaniel Porlock, who had been ashore December 24 and had distributed "a pocketful of trifles to the women and children who surrounded him wherever he walked."

On Christmas Day he wrote that a boatsman named Tyaana came aboard His Majesty's ship *King George* and brought him a present of some hogs and vegetables, "which I received and made him a return that pleased him very much." Christmas gifts had been exchanged for the first time in Hawaii.

ISLAND MINCE PIE

This recipe is based upon a mélange of fruit and is Hawaiian-inspired.

- 1   8-ounce jar red maraschino cherries, drained
- 1   8-ounce jar green maraschino cherries, drained
- 1   cup fresh, frozen, or canned pineapple chunks, drained
- ⅓   cup candied orange peel
- ¼   cup currants
- ½   cup seedless golden raisins
- ½   cup walnut pieces
- ½   cup sugar
- 2   teaspoons arrowroot
- 2   tablespoons rum
- 1   tablespoon milk
  Pastry for one 2-crust pie

Combine fruits and nutmeats. Mix sugar and arrowroot together and add to fruit and nuts. Stir to mix. Add rum. Pour mixture into prepared 9-inch pastry-lined pan. Cover with top crust. Brush milk lightly over this. Bake on bottom shelf in hot oven (425°) 30 to 45 minutes, until crust is a golden brown.

Makes one 9-inch pie.

MANGO PIE

This recipe is an old Hawaiian stand-by of Virginia
Nielsen McCall, who lived in the Hawaiian Islands for
four years while her husband was in the armed services.

½ cup sugar
2½ tablespoons cornstarch
2 tablespoons tapioca
5 or 6 mangoes, sliced like apples
½ teaspoon salt
¼ cup water
½ cup maple syrup
2 tablespoons lemon juice

Combine all ingredients except lemon juice. Bring to a
boil and cook two minutes. Cool. Add the 2 tablespoons
lemon juice, stir to blend, and pour into unbaked 9-inch
pastry shell.

TOPPING

6 tablespoons sugar
6 tablespoons flour
2 tablespoons butter or margarine
⅛ teaspoon salt

Mix together with fingers or pastry cutter until crumbly.
Sprinkle over top of pie.
Bake in a hot oven (400°) about 40 minutes.
Makes one 9-inch pie.

NATCHEZ PECAN PIE

When Mrs. O. T. Hagen, formerly of Natchez, Mississippi, gave me her plantation recipe for Pecan Pie twenty-
five years ago this favorite Southern pie was scarcely
known west of the Mississippi. Now I am sure it is in the

recipe files of thousands of cooks across this land of ours.

Quick and easy to make, it is a good choice when a luscious dessert is wanted to complete an otherwise simple meal.

   3 eggs
   1 cup Louisiana or dark corn syrup
   1 cup sugar
  ¼ teaspoon salt
 2½ tablespoons melted butter or margarine
 1½ cups pecans
   1 tablespoon milk
   1 teaspoon vanilla
   1 9-inch unbaked pastry shell
      Pecan halves

Beat eggs until thick and fluffy. Add syrup, sugar, salt, butter, pecans, milk, vanilla. Mix together. Pour into pastry shell. Place pecan halves in symmetrical or Christmas design on top of pie. Bake in hot oven (400°) 15 minutes, then reduce heat to moderate (350°) and cook for 15 to 20 minutes until filling is set and toothpick inserted in center comes out clean. Cool before serving.

Makes one 9-inch pie.

GRASSHOPPER PIE

The recipe for this rich and delectable frozen pie was given to me by Mrs. H. E. Andreson of Oakland, California, many years ago and is included here for its excellent flavor, festive color, and simplicity of preparation. It has another plus value too for one of the powdered commercial whipped topping mixes may be substituted for thick cream if a lower-calorie dessert is desired.

 16 Hydrox chocolate cookies, rolled fine
  4 tablespoons butter or margarine
  ¾ cup milk, heated
 24 large marshmallows

¼ cup green crème de menthe
2 tablespoons white crème de cacao
1 cup heavy cream or substitute

Roll cookies and filling to fine crumbs. Blend with melted butter and press into 9-inch pie plate, covering bottom and sides reserving 1 tablespoon for later use. Put into freezing unit. Combine hot milk with marshmallow in top of double boiler and cook over low heat until marshmallows are melted, stirring occasionally. Cool. Add ¼ cup green crème de menthe and 2 tablespoons white crème de cacao, stirring to blend thoroughly. Add a few drops of green coloring, if desired, for a deeper green color. Beat cream very stiffly, until it is almost at the butter stage. Fold into mixture with spatula, and pour over cooky crust. Sprinkle remaining cooky crumbs over top. Return to freezer until time to serve.

Makes one 9-inch pie.

PUMPKIN PIE

In Alice Morse Earle's *Customs and Fashions in Old New England* she gives an old recipe for making a "singular good Pumpion Pye." The ambitious and compound-sentenced concoction reads as follows:

"Take about halfe a pound of Pumpion and slice it, a handful of Tyme, a little Rosemary, Parsley and Sweet Marjoram slipped of the stalkes, and chop them smal, then take Cinamon, Nutmeg, Pepper, and six Cloves and beat them, take ten Eggs and beat them, then mix them and beat them altogether, and put in as much Sugar as you think fit, then fry them like a froiz, after it is fryed, let it stand til it be cold, then fill your Pye, take sliced Apples thinne rounde-wayes, and lay a row of the Froiz and layer of Apples with Currans betwixt the layer while your Pye is fitted, and put in a good deal of sweet butter before you close it, when the pye is baked take six yelks of Eggs, some White-wine or Vergis, and make a Caudle of this, but not too thick, cut up the lid and put it in, stir them well together whilst the Eggs and Pompions be not perceived and so serve it up."

Now we take Pumpkin Pie for granted and serve it with pride from October through the winter season. Choose from the old traditional recipes or the modern chiffon or ribbon pies, but don't overlook this old traditional favorite for holiday entertaining. You, like me, may find my grandmother's recipe for Pumpkin Pie more convenient than the one quoted above.

GRANDMA'S PUMPKIN PIE

- 1 cup sugar
- 1 tablespoon flour
- ¼ teaspoon salt
- 1 teaspoon ground ginger
- 1 teaspoon cinnamon
- ½ teaspoon nutmeg
- ¼ teaspoon ground cloves
- ⅛ teaspoon black pepper
- 3 eggs
- 2 cups mashed pumpkin
- 1¼ cups rich milk
  9-inch unbaked pastry shell

Mix together sugar, flour, and seasonings. Beat in eggs. Stir in pumpkin and milk, blending thoroughly. Pour into a 9-inch unbaked pie shell. Bake in a preheated hot oven (400°) 40 minutes or until toothpick inserted in center comes out clean. Cool.

Makes one 9-inch pie.

MOLASSES PUMPKIN PIE

Decrease sugar to ¾ cup. Add ¼ cup unsulfured molasses. Decrease milk to 1 cup. Prepare and bake as above.

PUMPKIN PIE II

        3 eggs
     1¾ cups canned pumpkin
        1 cup dark brown sugar
       ½ teaspoon ground ginger
       ½ teaspoon nutmeg
       ½ teaspoon cinnamon
       ½ teaspoon allspice
        1 teaspoon salt
        2 teaspoons grated orange rind
     1½ cups evaporated milk
        2 tablespoons margarine
           Unbaked 9-inch pie shell

Beat eggs slightly in mixing bowl. Stir in pumpkin, sugar, spices, salt, and orange rind. Warm milk and margarine, but margarine does not have to melt completely. Add to pumpkin mixture. Blend. Pour into unbaked pastry shell and bake in a preheated hot oven (400°) 30 to 40 minutes, or until it tests done (silver knife tip inserted in center comes out clean). Cool. Serve topped with whipped cream, if desired.

Makes one 9-inch pie.

Note: For variety, bake your pumpkin pie in a Walnut-Ginger Crust (page 208).

PUMPKIN RIBBON PIE

A rich variation of the traditional pumpkin pie.

CRUMB CRUST

4½ cups bite-size shredded rice biscuits, crushed to 1⅛ cups
¼ cup dark brown sugar, firmly packed
¼ teaspoon ground ginger
⅓ cup margarine, or butter, melted

Heat oven to 300°. Butter a 9-inch pie plate. Combine cereal crumbs, sugar, and ginger. Pour melted margarine or butter over crumbs. Mix thoroughly. Firmly and evenly pack into bottom and sides of pie plate—not on rim. Bake 10 minutes. Cool thoroughly.
Makes one 9-inch pie.

FILLING

1 cup canned pumpkin
1¼ cups sugar
½ teaspoon cinnamon
½ teaspoon nutmeg
¼ teaspoon ground ginger
¼ teaspoon salt
1 teaspoon vanilla
1 cup heavy cream or whipped cream substitute, whipped
1 pint vanilla ice cream

Combine pumpkin, sugar, spices, salt, and vanilla. Fold in whipped cream. Spread ice cream in bottom of cooled pie shell. Spoon in pumpkin filling. Cover and freeze 6 hours or overnight.
Makes one 9-inch pie.

RUM CHIFFON PIE

This is another Hawaiian Islands delicacy. Light and frothy, it is a welcome change after some of the heartier holiday selections. It comes from the file of my former secretary Madeleine Shaffer, whose friend Ruth Parker originated it in her Hawaiian Islands home.

    1   envelope unflavored gelatin (1 tablespoon)
    ¼   cup cold water
    3   eggs, separated
    1½   cups milk
    ¾   cup sugar
    ⅛   teaspoon salt
    3½   tablespoons Jamaica rum

Soften gelatin in water for 5 minutes. In a separate bowl beat egg yolks. Add milk, ½ cup of the sugar, salt, and cook over slow heat, stirring all the time. When mixture coats spoon, remove from heat, stir in gelatin, and cool until mixture thickens. Blend in rum. Beat egg whites until stiff, and gradually add remaining sugar, beating to blend. Fold into custard. Turn into a 9-inch baked pastry shell. Serve with whipped cream, or substitute topping, if desired.

Makes one 9-inch pie.

Note: For a thicker chiffon, add 2 scant teaspoons cornstarch combined with 2 tablespoons cold water during cooking period.

WEST INDIES FRUIT PIE

From St. Thomas in the Virgin Islands comes this exotic fruit pie, a real change in flavor from the usual Christmas pies. Make it with fresh fruit if available, but frozen or canned sweetened or unsweetened fruits will do almost as well.

1   cup cubed pineapple
2   pears, peeled and diced
2   bananas, diced
1   cup dried figs, cut fine
¼   cup grated coconut
½   cup light brown sugar, firmly packed
¼   teaspoon salt
1   tablespoon flour
    Grated rind and juice of 1 lemon
1   tablespoon milk
    Pastry for 2-crust, 9-inch pie

Combine pineapple, pears, bananas, figs, and coconut. Add brown sugar, salt, flour, grated lemon rind and juice and mix well. Pour into pastry shell, cover with pastry top, and seal edges. Brush top lightly with milk. Bake 15 minutes in a preheated hot oven (425°), then reduce heat to 350° and continue to bake 45 minutes longer. Serve hot with Rum Sauce.

Makes one 9-inch pie.

RUM SAUCE

2   tablespoons sugar
2   teaspoons cornstarch
¼   teaspoon cinnamon
2   tablespoons water
½   cup rum
1   tablespoon grated coconut

Combine sugar, cornstarch, and cinnamon. Add water and rum and mix well. Cook until sauce thickens, stirring constantly. Stir in coconut. Serve hot over pie.

There are many combinations of the fruit-filled tart. And you don't have to make your mincemeat unless you are so inclined. Bottled or packaged mincemeat, canned or frozen fruit can serve as the base for fillings for delicious little Christmas tarts. But it is fun to try your own additions such as extra brandy, minced tongue, or green tomatoes, ground nutmeats, and a dash of allspice or other spices—whatever your taste and smell dictate at the time of making.

EMPANADAS
Argentine Meat Tarts

This recipe from the Rafael Silberman home in Santa Rosa, Argentina, makes a "finger food" that is fun to serve.

    2   cups flour
    ⅔   cup butter
    ½   teaspoon salt
        About 6 tablespoons very cold water
    1   egg, beaten

Form a batter with the hands. Let it rest for half an hour. Stretch on floured surface and cut into circles with a biscuit cutter 3 to 4 inches in diameter.

For the filling:

    2   pounds ground beef
    ½   onion, cut thin
    2   hard-boiled eggs, chopped fine
    ½   cup raisins
    1   egg

Fry the ground beef and onion in some oil, adding the eggs and raisins. Put a spoonful of filling on each pastry circle, fold, and seal the edges, crimping to hold in place. Brush with beaten egg. Fry in deep oil or bake in a hot oven (425°) until golden brown.

Makes thirty 3- to 4-inch tarts.

SLOVENIAN TARTS

This excellent holiday tart came to me from Mrs. Marguerite Ingrim of Springfield, Illinois. A collector of recipes, Mrs. Ingrim is a booster for this tart. I am too.

½ cup margarine or butter
1 3-ounce package cream cheese
1 cup sifted flour
¼ cup currant jelly
1 egg yolk
2 tablespoons milk
¼ cup chopped walnuts

Cream margarine or butter with cheese until fluffy. Add flour and knead to make a smooth dough. Wrap and chill for several hours or overnight. Roll to ⅛-inch thickness and cut into 2-inch squares. Place ¼ teaspoon jelly on one corner of each square. Begin at jelly corner and fold edge, covering jelly completely. Roll the square diagonally. Shape into crescent. Brush with egg yolk mixed with milk. Sprinkle with nutmeats. Place on greased baking sheet and bake in hot oven (400°) for 10 to 12 minutes.

Makes 12 to 16 tarts.

CHRISTMAS U.S.A.

Early American Customs
and Celebrations

*"The main splendor was in the way food was cooked
in the home."*

—MARK TWAIN

MOST of the Christmas folk customs that we follow
came to America from the British Isles, Germany,
the Netherlands, the Scandinavian countries; others came
from Italy, Spain, and France. As in the motherlands,
Christmas celebrations in America were a blend of religious observances and secular practices from earliest
days.

Church attendance was a must. Gifts were not an important part of early observances. But hospitality—even
to strangers—the burning of the yule log, Christmas
games, fine food and drink were important aspects of the
American tradition.

Instead of featuring the boar's head bedecked with
"bays and rosemary" for the Christmas table, English
colonists in Virginia and elsewhere often substituted
roasted suckling pigs with apples wedged tightly in their
mouths, which they served with great style. They also introduced the "ancient sirloin," and mince pie, plum pudding, and other English desserts to American dinner

tables, and they decorated their homes for such occasions with trailing smilax garlands, mistletoe, holly, ivy, and other greens. They did indeed make Christmas in the New World elegant in the English manner.

Christmas was celebrated in Virginia from the beginning days of the nation, when it was still a subject of controversy in England. Harnett Kane tells us in *The Southern Christmas Book* that America's first clearly recorded Christmas ceremony took place in Virginia. "The area gave the embryo country its original observances and shaped them for generations to come."

Proud inheritors of the Christmas traditions of their native England, Virginians served fine foods and spirituous drinks in their new abodes. They added the eggnog, a cousin to the milk punch, and syllabub, as well as some new dishes which developed from the "yield of their lands." Kitchen gardens were bountiful, and many of the vegetables now used had their ancestral strains in those early gardens, including peas, celery, and pumpkin.

Great cakes, pies bulging with fruit fillings made aromatic with spices and spirits, steamed plum, fig, and other puddings appeared on American tables. Among the innovations were fried oysters for Christmas morning breakfast, journey or Johnny cake for every day, and Lady Baltimore Cake for gala occasions.

Oyster and sweetbread pies, sweet potato pie, Sally Lunn cake, crackling and batter breads, beaten biscuits, and a whole procession of old dishes adapted to available ingredients made their appearance at Christmas dinners, and as the country developed so did the excellence of the offerings on the menu.

There was a sense of ceremony from the first. In Williamsburg, the one-time capital of Virginia, the Christmas Eve ceremony of those early days is now re-enacted for all of us to enjoy. It centers around the blessing of the yule log—the biggest and best log to be found in the Virginia woodlands. As the huge log sputters its first few flames, guests are told that the fire was lighted in early American days to force the devil and evil spirits out of the home. The log was burned continuously throughout the Christmas season to protect all within the dwelling from the forces of evil. On Christmas Eve sprigs of holly were cast in the fireplace to rid the people of all disappointments. And everyone lighted his Christmas taper from the yule log to have a "piece of its magic."

From the first, Virginians combined worship with enjoyment of the day. About forty out of the original one hundred who had landed on Virginia's soil went to the little wooden church at Jamestown on their first Christmas in the New World (1607) and listened to the age-old message "For unto you is born this day in the City of David, a Savior, which is Christ the Lord."

A year later they had their first Christmas feast, thanks to the friendship of the Indians. They had gone to call on one of Chief Powhatan's sons, and he arranged a bountiful meal for them. The colonists were reported as saying "Never more merrie, nor fedde on more plentie of good oysters, fish, flesh, wild foule and good bread, nor never had better fires in England than in the warm smokie houses." A suitable Christmas meal but very different from the roasted peacock and other birds and pies of England, the boar's head, and the baron of beef of their yesteryears.

In 1746 the *London Magazine* declared of Christmas in the New World ". . . an universal Hospitality reigns; full tables and open Doors, the kind salute, the generous Detention, speak somewhat like the old roast-beef Ages of our Fore-fathers."

As more settlers arrived in the New World and new settlements were established, new Christmas customs were introduced. To many settlers in Louisiana, Tennessee, Texas and other areas, Christmas became a time for firing guns, setting off firecrackers, and making a lot of noise. In

the mountain areas the emphasis was on folk music, with
some beautiful carols developing there in celebration of
the Nativity. And in several parts of the South the Christmas morning hunt to hounds for a deer or fox was considered the way to usher in Christmas Day. This was a
favorite pastime of George Washington during his Mount
Vernon days.

Areas that we now know as Alabama, Maryland, Ken-
tucky, and West Virginia stressed the carnival aspect of
Christmas. This was a survival of medieval mummery,
with men wearing masks and costumes and gaily parading
the streets informally or going from house to house. Any
visitor was welcome in the holiday season in those times
and no one was ever turned away.

As in Europe, many homes featured Nativity scenes.
In the old South these were called "Christmas gardens."
Sometimes these scenes around the Christmas tree filled
an entire room, as they still do in certain rural parts of
Austria outside of Innsbruck, where beautiful hand-carved
wooden figures are generations old.

There was still a deep bond with times past. For instance in many parts of the South people believed in the
old Scandinavian and European legend of the power of
animals on Christmas Eve. They thought that animals
were vested with the power to speak in return for their

kindness in keeping the Christ Child warm by breathing on Him the night of His birth. It was also considered very bad luck for any human to try to understand the animals' conversation or to get too near to them on that night. It was particularly important for a human being to stay away from them at midnight. At that time the animals supposedly kneeled to worship the Infant. In the Blue Ridge country there was also a belief that on this night the bees buzzed a special song and that cows kneeled down to hear their song.

Gradually the Southern beliefs spread outward and westward as a fan spreads out from its narrow base. But these ideas were obliterated with the passage of time or greatly modified by other national groups that brought their special customs to colonial America.

The Dutch and Germans brought to New Amsterdam their concept of a dignified Saint Nicholas in regal robes riding his faithful white horse through the town, and then promptly changed the spelling of his name. And later, in 1823, when Clement Clarke Moore wrote "Visit from St. Nicholas," beginning " 'Twas the night before Christmas,"

he characterized the giver of gifts to children as a jolly old fellow with a round belly that shook "like a bowlful of jelly," and Santa Claus was here to stay!

The Germans also brought the idea of the Christmas tree to the new land. They weren't sure just how it had originated. Some thought that the old legend of Saint Boniface was its origin. In Henry Van Dyke's *The First Christmas Tree,* it was told how Saint Boniface, earlier known as Wynfrith, brought Christianity to Germany. Like other missionaries in other times and in other countries, Boniface returned to his adopted land only to learn that the eldest son of the chieftain Gundhar was to be sacrificed to the gods on Christmas Eve in front of a mighty oak tree. Boniface lifted an ax and with one mighty blow felled the oak to the ground, to show that the pagan deity was powerless.

The assembled throng was amazed, then asked Boniface to show them God. Pointing to a young evergreen tree that stood nearby, he said: "This is the word, and this is the counsel. Not a drop of blood shall fall tonight . . . This . . . shall be a home tree tonight. It is the wood of peace, for your houses are built of fir. It is the sign of endless life, for its branches are ever green. See how it points toward Heaven. Let this be called the tree of the Christ Child; gather about it, not in the wild woods but in your homes; there it will shelter no deeds of blood, but loving gifts and lights of kindness."

The wood from the fallen tree was used to build a little church and monastery, and the fir tree was cut and taken to Gundhar's great hall where it was set up for the observance of Christmas.

The first Christmas tree? We don't know. Some believed that Martin Luther introduced it one Christmas Eve when he supposely carried a little fir tree across the glistening snow to his home where he set it up to delight his wife and children. Lighting the tree with many candles gave him the symbolism he needed to tell the children the meaning of the Christ Child, the Light of the World. But there are no facts to document this legend, only that the Christmas tree was first used in Germany. The colonists from Germany brought it to America and many customs evolved around it—hospitality, children's parties, family gatherings. Ever since, its influence has spread, as the Christmas fir extends its branches seemingly to envelop mankind.

The Germans (and the Dutch) also brought a heritage of many Christmas foods with them. They popularized roast goose and cakes made from Old World recipes. As late as 1872, Captain Jack Elgin of west Texas had a Christmas meal that could be compared to some of the early European feasts in quantity and variety. It featured as many as fourteen different kinds of meat, each prepared differently. These included antelope, bear, prairie dog, possum, wild turkey, quail, and other birds.

German and Dutch settlers also introduced America to baked specialties, such as *Lebkuchen,* ginger cakes; almond peaks called *Mandelspitzen;* sand tarts; *Grischdagringel,* a Christmas fruit-dough ring garnished with whipped cream and assorted candied fruits; *Kuchen; Fastnachtkuchen,* doughnuts; and Shoofly Pie.

Seventeen Moravians who had left their native Bohemia (Czechoslovakia) to·seek a new life in America came to the Lehigh Valley and founded a little colony there. They set about to make a shelter to protect them from the oncoming winter, and completed it just before Christmas. They gathered in the log house with the adjacent stable to hold their first vigil in their as yet unnamed settlement.

The religious service with the sounds from the animals in their shelter made them reflect on the Christmas vigil some seventeen hundred years earlier in Palestine. It suggested a name for their new home—Bethlehem.

Ever since that first observance the Moravians have held a religious observance of the Nativity. Joyful songs, the ringing of bells, and the following of old customs are still important in the "Christmas city," and have become as famous as the Moravian baked specialties.

Now on the afternoon before Christmas a trombone serenade ushers in the Bethlehem, U.S.A., celebration. At a special Christmas Eve church service, huge trays laden with beeswax candles made by the women of the congregation are passed to those who have come to celebrate the Nativity, and each worshiper lights his candle and joins in singing:

"Behold a great heavenly sight
From Bethlehem's manger shining"

at the conclusion of which, mounds of Christmas cookies and mace-seasoned buns are served to the worshipers.

But Christmas was by no means universally celebrated in the New World in its early days. The New England Puritans would have none of it. During the first century of colonial life few days were set aside for pleasure. Survival was uppermost in the minds of those first settlers. The sacred days of the English Church were a "stench to Puritan nostrils," according to Alice Morse Earle in *Customs and Fashions in Old New England*.

Public celebrations were banned. The Puritans opposed any reveling or playing of games, any form of "mad mirth," as contrary to the religious observance. Of course the Church of England had long ago frowned upon too much revelry. But the Puritans forgot this, or chose to. The pattern in early New England was to spend Christmas as one would any other day, in work. William Bradford, a Pilgrim father and governor of the Plymouth colony, said: "Ye 25 day begane to erect ye first house for commone use to receive them [Pilgrims] and their goods."

By 1659 the colonists had come to hate the thought of Christmas. Any person who stopped work or feasted in any way was fined five shillings in an effort to "beate down every sprout of Episcopacie." However, when the Church of England established special Christmas services, law enforcers knew they were powerless against the growing sentiment in America to have Christmas recognized as a holiday, and to permit the individual to observe it as he wished.

Through the years the observance evolved with unique American embellishments. But one thing did not change: special recipes and menus were passed down from one generation to the next. As life became more sedentary, menus were made simpler and courses fewer in number, but the custom of baking traditional favorites continued in the United States as in other Christian lands in the month of December.

Today we find a great increase in the number of pre-made products offered on supermarket shelves and in commercial freezers to simplify Christmas baking. Apron strings are being loosened. Will this trend obliterate the regional specialties that have been characteristic of groups of various national origins? It is too soon to tell, but the many labor-saving mixes and methods do help young and old to become expert cooks and at the same time have time and energy to enjoy December parties.

Christmas in the White House

CHRISTMAS with our First Families in the White House has differed from family to family. One outstanding characteristic of these Christmases has been the emphasis on children. Whether the President was a widower like Thomas Jefferson, a bachelor like James Buchanan, or a beaming grandparent like Franklin D. Roosevelt or Dwight D. Eisenhower, the President of the United States has made Christmas a ceremonial for the young.

In the earliest years of the newly formed nation, before it had a fixed capital city, Washington and Lady Washington, as she was known at that time, received their guests in Philadelphia. When they entertained it was at rather formal affairs, for Washington was a man of dignity who unbent only within the family circle and with his grandchildren. He was a striking man as he moved through the drawing room, his hair powdered and carefully coiffed, and dressed in coat and breeches of black velvet, "white or pearl-colored vest, . . . silver knee and shoe buckles,

and a long sword with a glittering steel hilt and scabbard of polished white leather." The Washingtons saw to it that entertaining was done with a degree of elegance and that traditional foods from old England were served in new America.

Christmas Dinner at Mount Vernon was usually served at three o'clock in the afternoon. The general was punctual about his meals and liked his guests to be on time too. He was known to have said to tardy guests: "Gentlemen . . . I have a cook who never asks whether the company has come, but whether the hour has come."

Dinner was served in three courses and on two tablecloths. One cloth was removed between the first and second courses, and the fruit, nuts, and wine were served on a bare table. A handsome silver epergne graced the center of the table, and platters filled with meat and fish were arranged symmetrically around the table, with vegetables, condiments, gravies, and sauces.

Toasts concluded the dinner, and on one occasion the President was known to have toasted everyone by name, so that the ladies tarried unduly long!

A CHRISTMAS DINNER, MOUNT VERNON STYLE

Green Turtle Soup

White Fish in Madeira Sauce

Roast Beef and Yorkshire Pudding

Roast Pig   Boiled Leg of Lamb

Roast Turkey with Chestnut Dressing

Giblet Gravy

Hominy   Sweet Potatoes

Minted Peas   Buttered Celery

Cantaloupe Pickle   Cranberry Conserve

Mince Pie*   Apple Pie*   Cherry Pie

Snowballs*   Indian Pudding

Great Cake*   Plum Pudding

Nuts   Raisins   Fruit

Wines

*Recipe in this book.

MARTHA WASHINGTON'S GREAT CAKE

Perhaps our most famous holiday cake is Martha Washington's Forty-egg Cake, often called "Great Cake," which some say originated in her kitchen, but which is very similar to the old English Great Cakes.

Mrs. Washington's recipe reads this way:

"Take 40 eggs & divide the whites from the youlks & beat them to a froth. Start working 4 pounds of butter to a cream and put the whites of eggs to it a spoon full at a time until it is well work'd. Then put 4 pounds sugar finely powder'd to it in the same manner. Then put in the youlks of the eggs & 5 pounds of flouer & five pounds of fruit. 2 hours will bake it. Add one half ounce of mace, one nutmeg, half a pint of wine and some frensh brandy."

Now if you are not exhausted just from reading about it, you might use this recipe which is quite similar and which I worked out some years ago for one cake.

MARTHA WASHINGTON'S CHRISTMAS CAKE

½ pound golden seedless raisins
½ pound currants
½ cup citron
½ cup candied orange peel
⅓ cup candied lemon peel
¼ cup glazed pineapple, cut in small pieces
½ cup brandy or grape juice
½ pound (2 sticks) butter or margarine
1 cup sugar
5 eggs, separated
1 teaspoon lemon juice
2¼ cups flour
½ teaspoon soda
½ teaspoon mace

1   teaspoon cinnamon
¼   teaspoon nutmeg
2   tablespoons sherry

Cut up raisins, currants, and candied fruits, using scissors that have been dipped in water. Put in a bowl and pour in brandy. Cover and let stand overnight. Stir the next morning and add more brandy if fruit has become dry. Soften butter and slowly beat in half of sugar. Beat egg yolks until a light lemon color and slowly add the other half of the sugar. Combine. Add lemon juice and stir. Sift in combined dry ingredients alternately with sherry. Add fruit. Fold in lightly beaten egg whites. Bake in a greased and floured 10-inch tube pan or a 10 × 4-inch round mold, filling within 1 inch of top. Put a pan of water in bottom of oven. Bake in a moderate oven (350°) for 20 minutes. Reduce heat to 300° and bake 1½ hours more, depending upon size of baking pans. Test for doneness. Cool. Wrap in waxed paper and store in covered container (see below).

Makes one 5-pound cake.

Like other fruitcakes, Martha Washington's Great Cake may be glazed with hot corn syrup and water to hold nutmeats and candied fruit decorations in place. Let cool. Then wrap in cheesecloth sprinkled with brandy; wrap in foil. Store in a container until ready to serve. Make two to six weeks before use and "freshen" brandy sprinkling, if desired.

By 1800, when John Adams took over as President, Mrs. Adams was confronted with a cold and unfinished home away from her New England home. "No one room or chamber is finished" and hardly six rooms were furnished. Water had to be carried from a distance of almost six blocks and the Adamses kept thirteen fires going all day to attain a modicum of comfort. "I had much rather live in the house at Philadelphia," she said. However,

Abigail Adams put her New England practicality to work and somehow created an environment that met their personal and official needs. With no yard in which to dry the laundry, she turned to what was available inside the house. This is how the East Room became a drying room for laundry at one time in its proud history.

It was she who prevailed upon the President to inaugurate the custom of White House Christmas parties for the children. The rooms were lighted and heated as well as possible. The President and the First Lady received formally in the upstairs Oval Room, which was hung with garlands and boughs of greens, as they greeted the friends of their young granddaughter Suzanna. Cakes, punch and other refreshments were served. The children grew tired, as four-year-olds will, and it is reported that young Suzanna snatched a friend's doll and bit off its nose because the guest had thrown her new set of doll's dishes to the floor.

President Jefferson, who followed the Adamses in the White House, was a highly cultivated man, informal in dress, epicurean in food tastes. He hired a chef from France and introduced the capital to waffles from the Netherlands, French ice cream and pastries, and *pastas* from Italy. He became noted for his excellent European cuisine and imported delicacies.

At one of his holiday parties his six grandchildren wandered at will among the adult guests, and he called for his violin and delighted them with his impromptu playing.

The tradition of Christmas receptions spread over the capital city, in the government circles and others. Many came to Washington just for these Christmas-to-New Year gala affairs. Famous and distinguished residents opened their homes for these great occasions, while the less eminent went calling on them, with lists in hand, often going from place to place and sometimes to the homes of people they had never met, from the President's mansion down. Everyone was welcome during the holiday season—a carry-over from the old European custom of hospitality and welcome to anyone who might call at Christmas time. No thought was given to intrusion or to any threat to personal safety. Man was "bound" to man for the Twelfth Night period through religious observance and social custom.

A widower at this time, President Jefferson relied on his daughters, Martha and Maria, as his hostesses and upon Dolley Madison for advice and as a stand-by.

Presidents came and went from the Washington residence, but it was Andrew Jackson, "Old Hickory" of Tennessee, who gave new excitement to the children's celebration of Christmas in the White House. His wife's niece, Mary Emily Donelson, told of a tense week in 1835 among the children of the household.

There were four Donelson children and two children of Jackson's adopted son. It was to all of them that the President referred when an invitation to other young people was worded: "The children of President Jackson's family request you to join them on Christmas Day, at four o'clock P.M., in a frolic in the East Room."

His little relatives were beside themselves as Christmas Eve neared. Although Santa Claus, "the fat old saint of the Teutons," had not really established himself as yet in America, the White House children could talk of nothing else to the staff. Would he surely come? What would he look like? How would he know they were there?

The big, good-natured Mammy said that she wished they would stop their chatter, and that maybe the old man would sit at home and roast chestnuts in front of his fire if it was too cold to be out and about.

The gardener, recently arrived from the Black Forest, said he was sure Kris Kringle would come, although he thought it strange that there would be no decorated tree to greet him. Carita, a Mexican embroidery worker for the family, said she couldn't be sure about Santa Claus's visit. In her native Mexico children hung lamps on poles and bushes on Christmas Eve, and the next morning found presents left "by the Infant Jesus on His Way from

Heaven to the Virgin's arms." The coachman added another note. He remembered that in many parts of the world mischievous children who reached into their stockings for little gifts or candy and cookies discovered to their dismay only peach-tree switches with a label: To be applied when spanking has proved insufficient. How terrible, they thought!

The day before Christmas the President invited the children to accompany him in his carriage to deliver gifts to friends and to children of a local orphanage. He told them of his own bleak boyhood without family or gifts on Christmas and talked of the importance of remembering others in the holy season.

That evening the President invited the youngsters to his room to hang their stockings. Some borrowed oversized ones from the two-hundred-pound cook. Stockings were hung from the mantel, from curtain rings at the foot of Jackson's bed, one from the "boot jack carelessly left on Uncle's green leather armchair." One of the children persuaded the President to hang his own stocking. He agreed, commenting that he had waited almost seventy years to do such a thing.

Like all children before and after them, these children begged to be allowed to stay up on Christmas Eve. As in other homes across the land, permission was refused. They awakened the next morning to find their stockings bulging with cakes, candy, nuts, fruit, and in each, a shiny silver quarter. The President's sock was stuffed with a cob pipe, a tobacco bag, a pair of warm slippers, and other gifts. He seemed as pleased as the children at the thoughtfulness expressed toward him.

At four o'clock on Christmas Day the long-awaited party took place. It was held in the East Room, which was decorated with greens, flowers, and mistletoe for the occasion. There were games, singing, and dancing. Two hours later the doors of the dining room were opened and

the band played "The President's March" as the children entered in line, keeping time to the music.

There before them were the triumphs of the kitchen: frozen ices in the shapes of apples, pears, and vegetables; a little pine tree with toy animals around it; a reindeer pausing near a lake in which were little fish. Eyes focused on a pyramid of cotton "snowballs" covered lightly with starch. After the feasting, the children reached for the snowballs with unexpected results. When struck properly, each ball exploded, and the East Room in a moment was converted into an area of "snow" and smoke. A never-to-be-forgotten Christmas for all those present.

PECAN NUT CAKE

One of the festive cakes served for special occasions during James K. Polk's presidency was a Hickory Nut Cake. Since this nut is hard to get in some sections of the United States, I have substituted pecans. Of course the old recipe called for a butter batter cake, but an excellent-tasting cake can be made with a high quality margarine, or with a combination of butter and margarine if you want the butter flavor but want to cut down on the amount of solid fat in the recipe.

1   cup (2 sticks) margarine
2   cups sugar
4   eggs, separated
1   teaspoon lemon juice
3   cups flour
2   teaspoons baking powder
½   teaspoon salt
1   cup milk
1   cup pecans, chopped fine
1   teaspoon almond flavoring

Grease and flour a 10-inch tube pan, 4 inches deep. Cream margarine with 1 cup of the sugar. Beat egg yolks until light, add the remaining cup of sugar and beat until light and lemon colored. Then stir in lemon juice and mix to blend. Next sift dry ingredients together and add alternately with the milk. Stir in nuts and flavoring. Beat egg whites until light and able to form peaks, but not dry. Fold in lightly. Pour into a tube cake pan, and bake in a moderate oven (350°) about 1¼ hours. Use your favorite caramel or white frosting and sprinkle with nuts, grated coconut, or colored sugar crystals, or use Pecan Nut Frosting.

PECAN NUT FROSTING

1 cup sugar
½ cup cold water
2 egg whites
1 teaspoon vanilla
1 cup chopped pecans

Make a syrup of the sugar and water, cooking to the soft-ball stage (234° on your candy thermometer). Allow to cool while egg whites are beaten. Now pour the syrup in a steady stream onto the beaten egg whites, stirring the mixture until it is thick enough to spread over cake. Add flavoring at the very last before spreading on cake. Sprinkle top and sides of cake with chopped nuts.

Makes one 10-inch cake.

DOLLEY MADISON'S CARAWAY CAKE
(1968 version)

Dolley Payne (Todd) Madison of North Carolina has been depicted as the First Lady with the greatest flair for entertaining ever to grace the White House. In the 1964 edition of *The White House Cookbook*, Janet Halliday Ervin writes that Washington hostesses have been trying to recapture her spirit ever since.

Mrs. Madison loved people, parties, and projects, and had a flair for entertaining any month in the year. She became the leader of everything fashionable in Washington and continued her social career for more than forty years with few interruptions.

From a devout Quaker family, she had married James Madison when she was a young widow with one child—and was promptly "read out of" the Pine Street Meeting. Warmhearted and gay, she soon learned to adapt to her new life in Washington.

Washington Irving wrote of his Washington visit that she was "a fine, portly, buxom dame, who has a simple and pleasant word for everybody . . . but as for Jemmy Madison—ah poor Jemmy—he is but a withered apple-john."

As First Lady at forty-one, she introduced French gowns and feathered and bejeweled turbans and a kind of entertaining the capital had not previously known. She redecorated the White House in her favorite color of sunny yellow. Satins and damasks of the new color gleamed brightly.

With the help of an excellent steward, she introduced her guests to marvelous foods, superbly served. Of her fame as a provider of delectable foods she once said: "The Profusion of my table . . . arises from the happy circumstances of abundance and prosperity in our country."

One of her specialties was Seed Cake. A modern version can be made in a minimum of time with maximum results simply by using a white or yellow cake mix. Add 1 tablespoon caraway seeds, ⅛ teaspoon grated nutmeg, and ¼ cup brandy or sherry for an equal amount of the specified liquid. The result is cake of aromatic sweetness, worthy of your most honored guest.

It was hard for Mrs. James Monroe to emulate the glamorous Dolley Madison, and wisely she did not try. Rather she entertained in formal European style, serving French foods with a flair. Americans grumbled. English and French visitors were impressed with the quality of the Monroes' special entertaining.

It was Franklin Pierce of New Hampshire who first introduced a Christmas tree to the White House, in the 1850s. He had it installed for the enjoyment of his little guests from the Sunday School of the New York Avenue Presbyterian Church. The decorated "German tree" was by then receiving acceptance in this country.

When Benjamin Harrison became President in 1889, he and his wife brought with them her father, their son and daughter and their families. He proclaimed Christmas "the most sacred religious festival of the year" and said it should mean rejoicing for all. "We intend to make it a happy day . . . all the members of my family, representing four generations, will gather around the big table."

The President announced that people had a duty as Christians "to make merry" at this season and declared that in his own home he would have an old-fashioned Christmas tree.

Later, when the White House was the home of the gay and boisterous six children of Theodore Roosevelt, the President let it be known that he was strongly opposed to the use of evergreens for Christmas trees. An ardent conservationist, he felt that slashing down thousands of trees would injure the forests. His good friend Gifford Pinchot explained to him that the intelligent cutting of evergreens would not damage the forests but actually help them. Convinced of the logic of his friend's explanation, the President finally allowed his boys to have a tree in one of their rooms.

By the time the Calvin Coolidges were the First Family, in the early 1920s, the tree in one form or another was a fixture. The Coolidges had two large trees, one in the Blue Room and a second in an upstairs room. Later, using a raised platform, the family installed a manger scene with five or six evergreens behind it. In 1923 Calvin Coolidge pressed a button to light the first "national Christmas tree," which towered on the White House lawn.

New years and new administrations brought other changes. With Franklin D. Roosevelt's large family, a bubbling vivacity came to the holidays in the White House in the 1930s.

The Franklin Delano Roosevelts loved Christmas. Mrs. Roosevelt began planning for it each year as early as August. On her various trips away from Washington she tried to do a little shopping whenever she would manage it. Not only was her family list very large but she personally selected a gift for every child under sixteen years of age of the families of the White House staff. Wrapping and tagging these gifts stretched on for weeks before the December day when the President and Mrs. Roosevelt greeted staff members and their families. A handshake, an exchange of cordial greetings in the traditional way, a gift for each young person!

With her fine appreciation of people, it is only natural that Mrs. Roosevelt would take particular pains to express hospitality, and she developed many seasonal specialties.

One of her favorites was Swedish Cookies. She gave the recipe listed below to my dear friend Mrs. Laurence Merriam when she was her guest for tea in Yosemite Valley (Mr. Merriam was then superintendent of Yosemite National Park), and Mrs. Merriam has generously consented to its inclusion here.

MRS. FRANKLIN D. ROOSEVELT'S SWEDISH COOKIES

2   cups butter
1   cup sugar
1   egg
1   teaspoon flavoring
4   cups cake flour
    Egg yolk
2   tablespoons milk

Cream butter, add sugar. Add egg and flavoring, and lastly blend in flour. Chill. Turn out onto canvas-covered board or put between 2 pieces of waxed paper, roll thin, and cut with any shape cooky cutter. Brush with egg yolk mixed with 2 tablespoons milk, and decorate with coconut, cherries, colored candies, or nuts chopped medium fine. Place onto greased cooky sheet, and bake in preheated hot oven (400°) about 6 minutes until light brown.

Makes about 70 cookies.

With Dwight D. Eisenhower's election to the presidency young children returned once again to the White House, and during the Christmas season of 1955 a grandchild was born to the official family.

Mrs. Eisenhower, known affectionately to all America as "Mamie," was a First Lady of unusual charm and feminity. Like Mrs. Truman who preceded her, her paramount interest was her husband—his welfare and his comfort. She shied away from public involvement and was quite content to "leave it to Ike." During the thirty-seven years that she had served as an Army wife she had learned protocol that made her elevation to mistress of the White House a very easy one. She met with the staff heads of their seventy servants, indicating her wishes, but let them put these into effect with minimum interference. She liked everything carried out with care but was not overly interested in the details of White House housekeeping. Her primary concern was for the welfare of her husband and family.

With such family devotion, one is not surprised to learn that the Eisenhowers spent a "traditional American Christmas" in the White House. There were lots of cookies for grandchildren and guests.

Mrs. Eisenhower has generously shared her Sugar Cookies recipe, as listed below.

MRS. EISENHOWER'S SUGAR COOKIES

1½ cups flour
1   teaspoon baking powder
½   teaspoon salt
½   cup butter
1   cup sugar
2   egg yolks
1   teaspoon vanilla
1   tablespoon cream

Mix and sift flour, baking powder, and salt. Cream butter, add sugar slowly and cream until fluffy. Stir in well-beaten egg yolks and vanilla extract. Add sifted dry ingredients alternately with the cream. Chill for at least one hour, roll and cut in any desired shape. Sprinkle with sugar before baking. Bake in a moderate oven (375°) 10 to 12 minutes.

Makes about 36 cookies.

The John Fitzgerald Kennedys brought youthful charm and vigor to the White House in 1961. The third youngest President's wife in history, Jacqueline Bouvier Kennedy brought gentility, cultural interests, and a sturdy individualism to her new position as First Lady. "I will be, first, a wife and mother; second, the First Lady," she said with determination.

But she was shocked that so little of the nation's proud past was expressed in the furnishings of the White

House. They had become a hodgepodge collection from the thirty-four First Families that had previously lived there. She determined to correct this and formed a committee to work with her on the restoration of its interior. She carried her work to the country by showing the progress through a personally conducted television tour of the official residence. People were delighted.

Mrs. Kennedy left her mark as First Lady in other ways as well. She and her husband scored with their original entertaining. Dishes in the tradition of fine French cuisine, her preference, appeared on the menu more regularly than at any time since Thomas Jefferson's day.

Mrs. Kennedy has chosen a delicate French dessert, *Crème Brûlée*, to share with you. It is an elegant dessert for any special occasion and could be served during the holiday season with Mrs. Roosevelt's Swedish Cookies or Mrs. Eisenhower's Sugar Cookies as an accompaniment.

JACQUELINE KENNEDY'S CRÈME BRÛLÉE

- 3 cups heavy cream
- 1 1-inch piece of vanilla bean
- 6 tablespoons of sugar
- 6 egg yolks
  Brown sugar

In upper part of double boiler, heat three cups of heavy cream with a 1-inch piece of vanilla bean. In a bowl beat six tablespoons of sugar with six egg yolks until light and creamy. Take out the vanilla bean, and stir the warm cream into the yolks very carefully and slowly.

Return the mixture to the double boiler. Stir constantly over boiling water until the custard coats the spoon. Then put into a glass serving dish and place it in the refrigerator to set. When ready to serve, cover the top of the custard completely with brown sugar, using ½ cup or more. Place the dish on a bowl of crushed ice and place custard under broiler flame until sugar melts and caramelizes. Keep watching it, for the sugar will burn. Serve immediately. Crème Brûlée is often prepared and served in straight-sided, ovenproof individual baking dishes.

Serves six.

With President Johnson's elevation to the presidency, many changes took place in White House entertaining.

The elegant, rather formal affairs that were second nature to Jacqueline Kennedy gave way to a western brand of hospitality with a more informal atmosphere.

Claudia Alta (Taylor) Johnson, who was called "Lady Bird" by a doting nurse in her infant days and is to this day called "Bird" by her husband and close friends, brought altogether different qualities to her new role. Petite and feminine, Mrs. Johnson had been her husband's helpmate in all of his ambitions over a thirty-year period, and was experienced in the responsibility of combining social grace with political acumen.

Despite the many demands on her time Mrs. Johnson likes to give Christmas baskets of homemade bread, preserves, and sausage to her friends, and she has generously shared some of her favorite Christmas gift food recipes with me for you.

LBJ RANCH DEER MEAT SAUSAGE

A favorite recipe at the LBJ Ranch is for deer meat sausage. The finished product is recommended for late Sunday morning breakfast with scrambled eggs, hominy grits, hot biscuits, and boiling hot coffee. Or it can be served in hot biscuits for afternoon snacks.

- ½   deer
- ½   hog
- 25 ounces salt
- 20 ounces black pepper
- 8   ounces red pepper
- 2   ounces sage

Mix together for 200 pounds of sausage.

MRS. LYNDON B. JOHNSON'S WHITE BREAD

3   tablespoons solid shortening
½   cup sugar
1   cup scalded milk
2   yeast cakes dissolved in ¼ cup warm water
1   teaspoon salt
1   egg
4½   to 5 cups flour

Cream the shortening and sugar and pour scalded milk over this mixture. Allow yeast-water to cool and add to mixture. Using egg beater, add salt and the egg, beaten until light.

Add 4½ or 5 cups of flour 1 cup at a time, just enough so that the dough can be worked by hand.

Put dough in a large greased bowl—grease the top part of the dough and allow to rise until double in bulk. Cover with hot damp cloth several times—it takes about 2 hours for it to rise in a warm spot, not too near the stove. Toss on board with enough flour to keep it from sticking to the board, knead dough for 5 minutes, working outside edges in, kneading with the ball of the hand, repeating until dough no longer sticks to the board, is "bubbly" and puffs right back up. Divide into 2 equal loaves and place in two greased Pyrex baking dishes. Let dough rise again until double in bulk.

Bake at 450° for 10 minutes, reduce heat to 350° and bake for 30 more minutes (40 minutes in all). Bake until bread is brown and shrinks from the sides of dish. Remove and turn out to cool on wire tray. Slice when bread is cold. It can be baked a day or two before use—wrap in waxed paper. It is delicious sliced, buttered, and reheated.

Makes 2 loaves.

LBJ RANCH PEACH PRESERVES

  1 bushel of peaches
10 pounds of sugar

Peel and slice peaches into a large roasting pan. Build up layers of peaches with sugar in between and on top. Let this mixture set overnight. The next morning bring the peaches to a boil. As the peaches cook, a film will form and should be skimmed off the top; continue removing this film until the syrup is clear. Simmer for three to three and a half hours. Cook longer for thicker and darker preserves. Pour into sterilized jars and seal.

CHRISTMAS MENUS

G OURMETS discovered many years ago that the best recipes are not always found in cities or in the name restaurants. They are sometimes created in remote areas, like the "Joyous Coast" region along the Cane River in the northern part of Louisiana, famed for the abundance of game and fish for local use. In the old days it was not uncommon for one man to kill as many as two hundred wild fowl on a single outing. Naturally they were featured for days and weeks in plantation meals. Some were hung in the cold room for holiday use.

Fish were also abundant. It is said in Louisiana that an Indian could kill them with a bow and arrow faster than they could be brought in by another Indian. Some of these were said to weigh as much as thirty pounds. No wonder they were used in so many ways for Christmas entertaining!

Many colonial and ante-bellum landowners of large estates cherished recipes brought with them from France. The preparation of special dishes for great occasions was often supervised by the plantation mistress, but the skill of the plantation cooks, usually of African origin or descent, "gave a value to the cooking that exceeded the excellence of the original dish." François Mignon and Clementine Hunter wrote in *Melrose Plantation Cookbook* that at an early time in the history of Louisiana, menus in the great houses of the Joyous Coast blended ancient dishes of French origin with provincial ingredients. This combination of French cuisine, Louisiana products, and African artistry resulted in meat, vegetable, and game recipes little known to European gourmands.

A Christmas dinner in this part of the country in antebellum times might have appeared as listed below. (The asterisk following items in menus indicates that the recipe is in this book.)

ANTE-BELLUM PLANTATION CHRISTMAS DINNER

Game Soup

Boiled Bass à la Brin

Antelope Steak with French Sauce

Wild Turkey with Corn-meal Dressing

Cranberry Sauce   Giblet Gravy

Pickled Mangoes   Brandied Peaches

Potatoes *Marraine*   Candied Yams

Parsnips *Beignets*   Cauliflower *Piquante*

Apple Biscuits*

Plantation Plum Pudding with Sherry Sauce

Coffee

MAMA'S CHRISTMAS BREAKFAST

Smothered apples with frizzled bacon and airy golden-brown popovers were breakfast regulars in my childhood days when Christmas breakfast was a hearty meal. We ate heartily because there was no lunch on Christmas Day as dinner was served about two o'clock in the afternoon.

Orange Juice

Smothered Apples with Frizzled Bacon

Fluffy Scrambled Eggs with Shrimp or Mushrooms

Beef-Carrot-Potato Hash

Popovers*   Toasted English Muffins

Coffee

Chocolate

A HAWAIIAN CHRISTMAS BREAKFAST OR BRUNCH

Papaya Juice

Fresh Pineapple Boats

Banana–Macadamia Nut Pancakes

Island Syrup

Breakfast Sausages

Cranberry Coffeecake*

Beverages

A TRADITIONAL FRENCH CHRISTMAS DAY DINNER

A simple French dinner, like a more elaborate one, is served in many courses, as the French always serve one food to a course. This menu is printed through the courtesy of Mrs. A. W. (Marta Julin) Nielsen.

Paté de foie gras

(Goose liver)

Dinde avec farce aux marrons

(Turkey stuffed with chestnuts)

Salade verte

(Green salad)

Fromage

(Cheese—Roquefort, Camembert, Gruyère, etc.)

Bûche de Noël*

(Christmas Log—sponge roll with chocolate filling)

Burgundy or Champagne

A DANISH CHRISTMAS DINNER

Rice Porridge with Almonds

Roast Goose

Red Cabbage   Browned Potatoes

Pickled Beets   Pickled Cucumbers

Poppy Seed Rolls

Currant Jelly   Jams

Fresh Fruit, Assorted Nuts, *Kleiner*[1]

Candy   Danish Wreaths

Dried Figs

[1] See recipe for *Klenäter,* page 172.

A TRADITIONAL AMERICAN CHRISTMAS DINNER

Orange-Cranberry Shrub

Roast Turkey   Giblet Gravy

Bread Dressing

Mashed Potatoes with Dill

String Beans with Sautéed Mushrooms

Glazed Pearl Onions

Waldorf Salad in Cabbage Shell

Cranberry Sauce

Relish Tray—Olives, Pickles, Celery Hearts

French Rolls

Mince Pie*

West Indies Fruit Pie*

Beverages

DELICACIES FOR DIETERS

FOR MANY people the thought of having to observe any kind of diet restriction during the holiday season is unbearable. But it need not be, for food producers have developed excellent new products that make it possible to adapt many recipes to accommodate the dieter.

There are, of course, a great many kinds of controls. The simplest one is the low-calorie or weight watcher's diet—one that many follow month in and month out as insurance against overweight. This kind of diet presents no problems in December for you already know how much you can eat of what to keep yourself within desired weight limits. As you plan your own entertaining or accept holiday invitations, don't overeat at one party, decline everything at the next one. Take small servings of selected calorie-loaded rich Christmas specialties (no, don't try every cooky on that tray) and have few regrets when January 1 dawns.

This is a much better plan than going on a crash diet after a time of gorging, for a crash diet can present health hazards. Moreover, such a diet seldom leads to desired permanent results and you may find yourself having to crash-diet several times a year. This is considered a questionable practice by many leading physicians and should be undertaken only on the advice of your physician. *In fact, all dieting should be done under medical guidance so that your diet includes the essential nutrients for good health.*

Many people have to be on medically planned diets with restriction of total calories, sodium, carbohydrate, or fat intake. So perhaps a few suggestions on how to meet such needs will give a kind of helping hand to December activities in the kitchen.

The dieter who must restrict total calories has to eat less of high-calorie foods and has to watch the fat-rich foods. If sodium restriction is the problem, the use of salt in food must be moderated or eliminated. The range of sodium restriction is considerable and the desirable limits for the individual can be determined only under competent medical supervision.

Unfortunately most of the foods that form the backbone of the American diet are high in sodium content: meat, fish, eggs, and cheese—in fact most of the foods of animal origin. A little of them must be stretched a long way. But dietetic meat, fish, and egg products are now available. The Chicago Dietetic Supply House markets sodium-restricted shrimp, ham, bacon, and many other excellent-tasting dietetic foods. Other companies have specialties too.

Sometimes it is necessary to increase the protein content of the sodium-restricted diet while maintaining the low level of sodium. There is a marvelous commercial aid if this is the case. Your physician will probably tell you about it. It is called Casec and it comes from the laboratory of Mead Johnson. It is a powder derived from milk yet has a sodium content of only 1.4 milligrams per level packed tablespoon. It is almost tasteless and has a texture that blends easily with various ingredients in making baked specialties. It may be incorporated into yeast and quick breads, pie crusts, cakes, and some cookies. Its gift to you is better nutrition, since 1 level packed tablespoon also supplies approximately 17 calories and 4 grams of protein.

As to holiday delicacies, your safest procedure is to make them, unless you can find what you are looking for properly labeled for diet-restricted use. Unfortunately many bakery items are double offenders to sodium watchers, for they may contain both salt and leavening agents. One teaspoonful of baking powder contains approximately 408 milligrams of sodium and one teaspoonful of baking soda contains about 1232 milligrams of sodium. Then there is the salted butter too, which contains 49 milligrams of sodium in one teaspoonful.

Happily there are sodium-restricted baking powders that will give you excellent baked products and they may be used for all of the family or guests; it is not necessary to bake just for the dieter. And you can get by without adding salt in the making of baked specialties. If your physician has prescribed a salt substitute for your use, try it in small amounts in baking. Unfortunately, some salt substitutes impart a bitter taste to cooked foods and must be added after the food has been cooked—not practical in baked products.

You cannot rely on the squeeze of a lemon or the addition of wine or herbs to perk up many of your baked specialties because they would not give compatible flavor. But you can make pie crusts with fruit juice if you strongly object to the omission of salt in the basic recipe. Orange juice crust with a tart cranberry filling can be served proudly to your most honored guest, as it has a good texture and pleasing flavor in addition to being considerate of restrictions.

Fresh fruit pies are an excellent choice for this diet for, bless them, fruits are low in sodium content. Some canned fruits, however, do have salt added, so read labels if you must curtail sodium in the diet.

Eggs must be limited, particularly the white, in sodium-controlled diets. And the egg yolk must be limited in the fat-controlled diet.

Lately there has been increased emphasis on limiting not only total fat intake but also saturated fat included in the diet. The purpose of the fat-controlled diet is to lower total fat intake and the cholesterol content of the blood. Of course all of us have some cholesterol in our bodies and in the blood, but in some people the amount is higher than average. It may accumulate along the walls of the blood vessels and clog or narrow their openings so that the heart, brain, or other organs may suffer or perish from insufficient blood. And in some cases the blood vessel closes entirely.

It would be relatively easy to proceed with menu planning for fat restriction if it were possible to restrict just the foods and ingredients that contain cholesterol. However, the body can also manufacture cholesterol from the fats we, eat. Therefore a physician sometimes finds it necessary to limit both the amount of fat and the kind of fat a patient may eat.

The emphasis is now on reduction of total fat consumption, increasing the amount of unsaturated fat while decreasing the saturated fat to attain a two to one ratio. Fats and oils contain hydrogen in varying amounts. If the fat or oil has all the hydrogen it can contain, it is called a saturated fat. If it can take on additional hydrogen, it is called an unsaturated fat—and the more hydrogen it can absorb, the higher the degree of unsaturation.

Usually the hardness of the fat is the clue to its saturation. Fats that are solid at room temperature are generally high in saturated fat. These include meat fats, both visible and invisible, butter, margarines unless specially processed, lard, most vegetable shortening, and egg yolks. Fats that are liquid at room temperatures, vegetable and fish oils, are highly unsaturated. Coconut oil is an exception: it is highly saturated.

Food processers have gone to work to help you have more interesting meals if fat must be controlled. But before I mention some specifics let us continue with just a few of the additional curtailments. Chocolate should be avoided and cocoa used in your recipes as it is low in fat. Whole milk is not for you if saturated fat is limited, but nonfat milk or powder can be used in almost every one of your baked specialties with satisfactory results. Some non-dairy creams may be used, but you will have to become a label reader to choose wisely, for many of these contain coconut oil and therefore should not be used.

In making fat-controlled Christmas delicacies it is essential to use nonfat milk; egg white rather than the whole egg in baked products; vegetable oil or margarine high in polyunsaturated fat rather than butter or lard. It is not very hard to accomplish this with a little planning ahead.

Don't become discouraged, because there are many excellent commercial products that may be used. Angel cake and angel cake mixes of various flavors other than chocolate are fat free or very low in fat and may be used quite generously on this diet.

Some frostings are permissible, such as Fluffy White (Betty Crocker and Pillsbury), Lemon Fluff and French Vanilla (Betty Crocker), Fluffy Orange and Fluffy Pink (Pillsbury), Cream White (Swel) and others which do not contain fat. They are real time savers and give excellent results. Of course you will have to shun the chocolate and coconut frostings because of their high saturated-fat content. When a commercial frosting mix calls for the addition of milk, the equivalent amount of nonfat milk and water plus 1 teaspoon allowed oil for each half cup may be substituted.

Some commercial pie fillings, chiffon and others, may be used providing they do not contain coconut oil.

There are many excellent acceptable margarines now available as pointed out in an earlier section. These are a real boon to your Christmas baking. But some of the hydrogenated vegetable shortenings, although an improvement on the old, are not within the standards as set for oils, according to the California Heart Association (*Available Products for the Controlled Fat Diet*).

Those on calorie restriction or on the diabetic diet will have to avoid fruits' canned with sugar and use only the water-packed varieties. There are many fine packs for this use—Monarch, S & W Dietetic, Tillie Lewis, Dietetic, Blue Boy, Featherweight (Cellu) of The Chicago Dietetic Supply House, and many others.

Your physician will advise you as to the sugar substitute he prefers for your need. For many years I have worked with Calcium Sucaryl (Abbott Laboratories) and find it very satisfactory. This sugar substitute contains no calories or sodium. With it you can get a natural sugarlike flavor without adding to your calorie intake. There is no bitter aftertaste to this product, a double blessing. It comes in liquid and tablet form. One tablet, or ⅛ teaspoon liquid, is equal to about 1 level teaspoon sugar. Be sure to designate the kind of Sucaryl you want when you buy it, for Abbott makes both a Calcium Sucaryl for sodium dieters and a Sodium Sucaryl, a saccharin suitable only if there are no sodium restrictions. Other excellent sugar substitutes that I have used include Sweeta and Sweet'n Low, both giving acceptable results.

Nuts have to be limited or excluded from many special diets. They are high in calories and fat so are red-flag items for calorie counters and those on the diabetic diet. Except for roasted salted nuts, all of them may be used as allowed on the sodium-controlled diet. English and Black walnuts are preferred for fat-controlled diets where high linoleic acid content is desired. Limited quantities of Brazil nuts, peanuts, almonds, pecans, pistachio and pine nuts may also be included, but only if they are dry-roasted or untreated. Commercially fried or roasted nuts are not allowed on this diet because saturated fat is used in their preparation.

Aside from all of the excellent dietetic foods and the allowable regular ones, one of your best helpers can be the home freezer. Use it like a savings account in the bank, an insurance against future need. So used, it can give variety in your menus, save dollars in your food expenditures, because you can take advantage of sales prices to stock up on special items, and it can save energy.

To help you, take the given typical Christmas dinner that can be adapted relatively easily for the fat-controlled, low-calorie, diabetic, and sodium-controlled diets so that everyone in the family and guests with special needs may eat well and enjoyably on Christmas Day.

Make cranberry sherbet, bread dressing, and pies ahead of use and store in freezer. Stuff turkey just before roasting, and if there is leftover dressing, do scoop it out to store.

A Traditional American Christmas Dinner Adapted for Special Diets

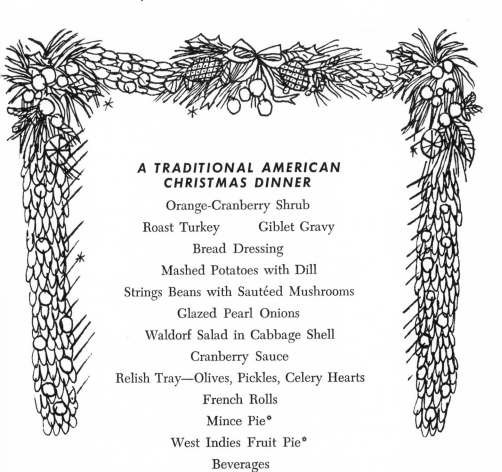

A TRADITIONAL AMERICAN CHRISTMAS DINNER

Orange-Cranberry Shrub

Roast Turkey   Giblet Gravy

Bread Dressing

Mashed Potatoes with Dill

Strings Beans with Sautéed Mushrooms

Glazed Pearl Onions

Waldorf Salad in Cabbage Shell

Cranberry Sauce

Relish Tray—Olives, Pickles, Celery Hearts

French Rolls

Mince Pie*

West Indies Fruit Pie*

Beverages

ORANGE-CRANBERRY SHRUB

For each serving: Fill sherbet glasses with 3 ounces orange juice and small scoop of cranberry sherbet. Serve with crisp cheese crackers or toasted Norwegian *Flatbrød,* if desired.

To Adapt the Recipe

Fat-controlled diet Prepare as directed and serve with crackers without added fat. Negligible fat content.

Low-calorie diet Serve with just one cracker. About 100 calories per serving.

Diabetic diet Substitute tomato juice. One serving equals 1 "A" vegetable exchange; count crackers toward bread exchanges.

Sodium-controlled diet Prepare as directed; serve with low-sodium crackers.

ROAST TURKEY

Before roasting, make a slit in breast of turkey and force into it a thin layer of celery leaves and a thin slice of onion for added flavor richness. Brush with margarine and white table wine, if desired, and bake on rack. Top with aluminum foil, if desired, but allow drippings to drip into pan.

To Adapt the Recipe

Fat-controlled diet Trim excess visible fat from turkey before roasting. Do not serve dieter skin or slice next to it.

Low-calorie diet Follow fat-controlled plan and baste only with approved margarine.

Diabetic diet No changes required.

Sodium-controlled diet Do not salt turkey before roasting and use only onion slices as suggested for flavor enrichment. Use foil wrap to avoid basting. Approximately 23 milligrams sodium per ounce of light meat, cooked. Approximately 28 milligrams sodium per ounce of dark meat, cooked.

GIBLET GRAVY

Make in usual way to have 6 cups liquid (gravy).

To Adapt the Recipe

Fat-controlled diet Boil only neck in water with a sliced onion and a few celery stalks, omit giblets as organ parts are high in cholesterol. Add a little highly unsaturated-fat margarine, if desired. Put a chunk of ice in drippings to solidify fat to be removed. Approximately 3 grams fat per ¼-cup serving.

Low-calorie diet Do not use turkey drippings in making gravy unless you thoroughly drain fat from pan drippings. Any thickening added to drippings increases calorie intake so limit amount of gravy to ¼ cup. Approximately 45 calories per ¼-cup serving.

Diabetic diet Prepare in usual way. One serving (½ cup) equals ½ meat, ½ bread, and 1 fat exchange.

Sodium-controlled diet Omit salt. Season with salt substitute and ½ teaspoon white table wine. Approximately 9 milligrams sodium per ¼ cup.

BREAD DRESSING

Make in usual way. Plan on 6 cups stuffing for a 12- to 16-pound turkey.

To Adapt the Recipe

Fat-controlled diet Sauté onions-celery (mushrooms, if used) in highly unsaturated-fat margarine. 5 grams fat per ½-cup serving.

Low-calorie diet Choose dressing or potatoes, not both. Prepare stuffing as directed above for fat-controlled diet, using only 1 teaspoonful of margarine. 100 calories per ½-cup serving (approximate value).

Diabetic diet Prepared as directed in fat-controlled diet. One serving equals 1 bread and 1 fat exchange.

Sodium-controlled diet Use unsalted margarine. Do not use packaged (salted) mix but make your own dressing from unsalted bread (if so specified on diet list), flavor-enriched with poultry seasoning or savory, thyme, white pepper (never black please, for poultry), and parsley. 5 milligrams sodium per ½ cup dressing if prepared with unsalted bread, unsalted margarine, and 1 tablespoon chopped mushrooms; 121 milligrams sodium if prepared with regular bread and mushrooms.

MASHED POTATOES WITH DILL

Allow 1 medium potato per person and prepare in usual way, adding a sprinkling of chopped fresh dill to taste after blending potatoes with milk, margarine, and other seasonings.

To Adapt the Recipe

Fat-controlled diet   Use nonfat milk and ½ teaspoon vegetable
    oil. 1 gram fat per serving.
Low-calorie diet   Prepare as above.
Diabetic diet   Prepare a small potato and proceed as above.
    One serving equals one bread and two fat exchanges.
Sodium-controlled diet   Omit salt. Approximately 2–3 milli-
    grams sodium per serving, without milk addition.

STRING BEANS WITH SAUTÉED MUSHROOMS

For each ½-cup serving, allow 1 tablespoon sautéed
sliced mushrooms and ¼ teaspoon margarine, ¼ teaspoon
lemon juice, ⅛ teaspoon sugar. Prepare in usual way.

To Adapt the Recipe

Fat-controlled diet   Omit margarine, unless highly unsaturated,
    and substitute corn or safflower oil. Approximately 1
    gram fat in 1 serving with margarine or oil.
Low-calorie diet   Prepare as outlined. Fat may be omitted if
    necessary. Approximately 21 calories without margarine
    or oil.
Diabetic diet   One serving equals ½ vegetable "A" exchange
    and ¼ fat exchange if oil is increased to 1 teaspoon.
Sodium-controlled diet   One serving prepared without salt
    equals approximately 4 milligrams sodium.

GLAZED PEARL ONIONS

Prepare glaze (for 6) with 2 tablespoons vegetable oil, pepper, 2 tablespoons sugar, ½ teaspoon fresh grated nutmeg.

To Adapt the Recipe

Fat-controlled diet One serving equals approximately 5 grams fat and a trace of saturated fat.

Low-calorie diet Serve plain, omitting the glaze. One serving equals approximately 30 calories.

Diabetic diet Omit glaze. One serving equals 1 serving "B" vegetable exchange.

Sodium-controlled diet One serving prepared without salt equals approximately 10 milligrams sodium.

WALDORF SALAD

Allow ½ medium apple unpeeled and cubed, 1 tablespoon chopped celery, 2 halves of walnut meats, and 1 tablespoon mayonnaise per serving.

To Adapt the Recipe

Fat-controlled diet Make mayonnaise with egg whites instead of whole eggs. One tablespoon equals approximately 14 grams fat.

Low-calorie diet Omit mayonnaise and nutmeats; use low-calorie dressing. If regular mayonnaise is used make it with egg whites instead of whole eggs. About 65 calories per serving with mayonnaise and nuts, about 37 calories per serving without mayonnaise and nuts.

Diabetic diet Omit sugar from mayonnaise; omit nuts. One serving equals 1 fruit exchange and 1 fat exchange with 1 teaspoon mayonnaise.

Sodium-controlled diet Omit celery and use only unsalted (special dietetic or homemade) mayonnaise. If mayonnaise is made with egg whites, one tablespoon equals 3 milligrams sodium per serving; if it is made with egg yolks, one tablespoon equals approximately 1 milligram sodium.

CRANBERRY SAUCE

To Adapt the Recipe

Fat-controlled diet 1 tablespoon equals a trace fat.
Low-calorie diet 1 tablespoon equals 25 calories.
Diabetic diet Omit unless made with artificial sweetener.
Sodium-controlled diet 1 tablespoon contains a trace sodium.

RELISH TRAY

To Adapt the Recipe

Fat-controlled diet 3 small ripe olives equal approximately 2 grams fat.
Low-calorie diet ½ large carrot equals approximately 10 calories.
Diabetic diet ½ large carrot (½ cup) equals 1 "B" vegetable exchange.
Sodium-controlled diet ½ large carrot equals approximately 12 milligrams sodium; 1 large outer stalk celery equals approximately 50 milligrams sodium; 2 small ripe olives equal 127 milligrams sodium.

FRENCH ROLLS
(1½ ounces, cooked weight)

To Adapt the Recipe

Fat-controlled diet   One roll is normally fat-free.
Low-calorie diet   One roll equals approximately 105 calories.
Diabetic diet   One roll equals 1½ bread exchanges.
Sodium-controlled diet   Use unsalted bread sticks.

MINCE PIE

One pint Green Tomato Mincemeat* made with apples, suet, light brown sugar, sun-dried raisins, and spices will make a 9-inch pie.

To Adapt the Recipe

Fat-controlled diet   Omit suet. One-twelfth serving equals 1 gram fat, a trace unsaturated fat in filling; 11 grams fat per serving of pie made with Vegetable Oil Pastry (page 206), using 2 teaspoons vegetable oil.
Low-calorie diet   Use 1/12 pie per serving. One serving made without suet and with 2-crust Vegetable Oil Pastry (page 206) equals approximately 443 calories.
Diabetic diet   1-inch section of a 9-inch mince pie 932 grams in weight equals 1 slice bread, ½ fat exchange, or 1½ servings fruit, ½ fat exchange.
Sodium-controlled diet   With unsalted crusts made of Vegetable Oil Pastry (page 206), one serving will equal approximately 9 milligrams sodium.

* See page 213.

WEST INDIES FRUIT PIE*

To adapt the Recipe

Fat-controlled diet Use Vegetable Oil Pastry (page 206). Omit coconut. One serving ($\frac{1}{12}$ pie) equals approximately 7.5 grams fat, 2 teaspoons vegetable oil.

Low-calorie diet Use $\frac{1}{12}$ pie per serving. One serving made with Vegetable Oil Pastry (page 206) equals approximately 289 calories.

Diabetic diet If used, must be made with unsweetened fruits only. It would be better to substitute pumpkin pie (1-inch section of a 9-inch pie, 32-gram weight), which equals 1 serving fruit, 1 fat exchange, or other allowable dessert.

Sodium-controlled diet Use Vegetable Oil Pastry (page 206), omitting salt. One serving (⅙ pie) equals approximately 20 milligrams sodium.

Christmas delicacies for the dieter should be planned and prepared ahead of time. Let your freezer work for you to permit early preparation according to the special needs of your dieter.

Christmas breads may be used in limited amounts for the fat-controlled diet if made at home with approved margarine or oil. Most of them should be skipped by the weight watcher and when eaten, not more than one slice per meal. The diabetic must avoid sugar-rich sweet breads but may use a popover for special occasions and nut or banana breads if made with little or no sugar.

Cakes, cookies, and calories have a natural affinity for one another, so must be used carefully and only as allowed on all diets.

For fat-controlled diet, plain angel food cake is an excellent choice, and cookies made with special margarine

* Without Rum Sauce. See page 230.

and white of egg. Meringue shells, some tortes and "kisses" are happy choices here. Chocolate should not be used because it is high in saturated fat, but cocoa may be substituted for it in many Christmas recipes. Bakery products in general must be bypassed in favor of home products.

The diabetic also must shun most Christmas baked specialties because of their calorie content but may eat, with the physician's approval, plain, pound, or sponge cake.

One tenth of an average sponge cake may be exchanged for 2 slices of bread.

One 3 × 2 × ¾-inch slice plain cake may be exchanged for 2 slices bread and 1 teaspoon butter.

One 2¾ × 3 × ⅝-inch slice poundcake is equivalent of 1 slice of bread and 1 teaspoon butter.

One 1¾-inch cupcake without icing is the equivalent of 1 slice of bread.

Of course these exchanges should not be used too often, but your doctor will tell you about this.

Christmas sweet breads, cakes, cookies, and pies made without salt may be used in the sodium-controlled diet with the consent of the physician. Many of the recipes in this book may be made without salt. Care must be used in amount of egg (particularly egg white) used because of high sodium content.

For detailed help on calorie, fat, and sodium control in the diet, see *The Fat and Sodium Control Cookbook* by Alma Smith Payne and Dorothy Callahan.* For recipes and information on the diabetic diet see *A Cookbook for Diabetics,* published by the American Diabetes Association.

* Published by Little, Brown & Company, 1965.

Table of Equivalents

Butter

For 1 cup, use 1 cup (preferably polyunsaturated) margarine

Chocolate

For 1 ounce (1 square) chocolate use 3 to 4 tablespoons cocoa and 1½ teaspoons acceptable margarine

Egg

For one whole egg use 2 whites. 1 egg white equals 2 tablespoons; 1 egg yolk equals 1 tablespoon

Flour

For 1 cup cake flour use ⅞ cup all-purpose flour

Honey

For 1 cup honey use 1¼ cups sugar plus ¼ cup liquid

Milk, whole

For 1 cup milk, use 1 cup water plus 3 tablespoons sifted nonfat milk powder plus 2½ teaspoons margarine or acceptable oil, if desired.

Nuts, shelled

Almonds: 1 pound equals 3 cups blanched
Pecans, halved: 1 pound equals 4½ cups
Walnuts, halves, English: 1 pound equals 4½ cups

 Standard Measures

Dash	=	less than ⅛ teaspoon
3 teaspoons	=	1 tablespoon
4 tablespoons	=	¼ cup
16 tablespoons	=	1 cup
1 cup	=	½ pint
2 cups	=	1 pint

Content of Cans

CAN SIZE	AVERAGE CONTENT	
No. 300	1¾ cups	3 to 4 servings
1 tall	2 cups	4 servings
303	2 cups	4 servings
2	2¼ cups	4 to 5 servings
2½	3½ cups	6 to 7 servings
3	4 cups	8 servings
10	12–13 cups	24 servings

Oven Temperatures

	ALL TEMPERATURES ARE FAHRENHEIT		
Very slow oven—	250°	and	275°
Slow oven—	300°	and	325°
Moderate oven—	350°	and	375°
Hot oven—	400°	and	425°
Very hot oven—	450°	and	475°
Extremely hot oven—	500°	and	525°

General Index

The General Index does not contain recipes or foreign terms, which are given separate indices of their own.

Index of Foreign Terms

Recipe Index

English translations of recipe names appear in this index. For original names, check Index of Foreign Terms.

ABOUT THE AUTHOR

ALMA SMITH PAYNE, a Californian by birth and by choice, was active in public education at the state and local levels before turning to full-time writing. Among the cookbooks she has written are *The Fat and Sodium Control Cookbook, The Low Sodium Cook Book,* and the revised edition of *Young America's Cook Book,* with Dorothy Callahan. She is also the author of *Discoverer of the Unseen World: A Biography of Antoni van Leeuwenhoek,* and *Partners in Science;* with her son Robert Warner Chambers, of the faculty of the New York University School of Medicine, she wrote *From Cell to Test Tube.* A member of the American Home Economics Association, she is a tireless worker in nutrition for the California Heart Association. Married to William R. Ralston, Agriculturist Emeritus of the University of California, she enjoys holiday entertaining in their home in Orinda, California.